GATEWAY *to*
THE EPICUREANS

GATEWAY *to*

THE EPICUREANS

Epicurus, Lucretius,
and Their Modern Heirs

**Edited, Translated,
and with a Preface by**

SPENCER A. KLAVAN

REGNERY
GATEWAY

Regnery books may be purchased in bulk at special discounts for sales
promotion, corporate gifts, fund-raising, or educational purposes. Special
editions can also be created to specifications. For details, contact the Special
Sales Department, Regnery, 307 West 36th Street, 11th Floor, New York,
NY 10018 or info@skyhorsepublishing.com.

Regnery Gateway® and Regnery® are imprints of Skyhorse Publishing, Inc.®,
a Delaware corporation.

Visit our website at www.regnery.com.

Please follow our publisher Tony Lyons on Instagram @tonyisuncertain.

10 9 8 7 6 5 4 3 2 1

Cataloging-in-Publication data on file with the Library of Congress

ISBN: 978-1-68451-516-5
eISBN: 978-1-68451-564-6

Printed in the United States of America

Contents

We Are All Epicureans Now

A philosophy is a way of life. So it seemed, at least, to the Epicureans and their rivals among the Stoics, the Skeptics, and the other Athenian philosophical "schools" of the Hellenistic Period (323–32 BC). They were not just competing to win over prospective students by demonstrating their intellectual superiority. They were also advertising the psychological benefits of certain daily practices and the good sense of a particular outlook. At the time, no one would have expected the Epicureans to corner the lifestyle market in terms of either numbers or influence. But in a very real way, though we often don't recognize it, the core principles of Epicureanism have become deeply embedded in the psyches of modern Westerners. Epicureanism is not just *a* way of life: it is *our* way of life.

In the short term, Stoics went mainstream while Epicureans remained mostly on the fringes. As Rome grew exponentially beyond its original borders, its elite increasingly set the terms of politics and culture all over the Mediterranean. Stoicism's bracing moral rigor had just the flavor of austerity and hardihood that appealed to Roman sensibilities. Epicureanism did win some noteworthy converts among the Roman upper crust, including on both sides of the civil war that led to Julius Caesar's rise. But Epicureans tended to favor a delicate withdrawal from politics, which was one of the things that rendered them suspicious to Romans of a more traditional cast of mind and made Epicurus an unlikely life coach for the conquerors of the world.[1]

In the long term, Epicurean assumptions have triumphed so entirely we often don't know they're there. They are simply part of the air we breathe, taken for granted in movies and magazine articles: everything is made of atoms, and the ideal life is one of serenity and well-being. In the ancient world these were outlandish proposals, requiring vigorous defense by way of elaborate argumentation. Today they are the starting points of self-help blogs and wellness routines. True, Stoicism has recently had a modern renaissance among online influencers and high-powered executives, inspiring massive Reddit forums and bestselling books.[2] But Epicureanism *needs* no modern renaissance, because it is already taken for granted practically everywhere. Ancient Epicureanism was practiced among privileged eccentrics and sophisticates. But a modern Epicurean revival would be utterly banal, consisting of unremarkable people living the way most others do.

---

1   The most famous Roman critique of Epicureanism—as morally lax, intellectually bankrupt, and politically disastrous—is to be found in the works of the republican statesman Cicero, especially his *Laws* and *De Finibus*. By contrast, the Stoics were so popular with the Romans as to claim an emperor—Marcus Aurelius—among their number.

2   See my foreword to *Gateway to the Stoics* (Washington, DC: Regnery, 2023).

"Our modern philosophers are all the low groveling disciples of Epicurus," griped John Adams, thinking perhaps of his erstwhile friend and rival Thomas Jefferson, who would at one point proclaim himself an Epicurean.[3] Resentment and contempt aside, Adams was hitting on a profound insight about what was then a relatively recent sea change. Today his observation is so true we don't even realize it, and Epicureanism has taken such a powerful hold on our imaginations that we hardly know it counts as a philosophy at all. It seems to us to be simply the way things are. It is therefore an exercise in self-understanding to study its history and its principles, to see it not simply as a default position but as a set of arguments, a way of life chosen among others. Learning about Epicureanism means learning to recognize ourselves.

◆ ◆ ◆

The story begins, not with Epicurus, but with an elusive sage named Democritus. He came from the Greek frontier town of Abdera in the wildlands of Thrace, a precarious region situated uneasily between mainland Greece and the Ionian outposts of Asia Minor (now Turkey). The native tribes of Thrace roved menacingly between the Danube and the Black Sea; they originally had no common identity or leader, though they were at one point collectively incorporated into the Persian empire and then loosely

---

3 John Adams to John Rogers, February 6, 1801. National Archives. https://founders.archives.gov/documents/Adams/99-02-02-4799. Thomas Jefferson to William Short, October 31, 1819. National Archives. https://founders.archives.gov/documents/Jefferson/03-15-02-0141-0001. I am indebted to Richard Samuelson for his expertise and intellectual generosity regarding all things John Adams.

united into the "Odrysian kingdom." Abdera itself, once an embattled Greek colony, came under Athenian protection in the Delian League. It was prosperous by the time Democritus was born in the mid-400s BC, but it bore scars left by Thracian shock troops and Persian taskmasters.[4]

Wherever he went, Democritus carried with him a certain whiff of the wild and exotic—it was rumored that he had spent time among the naked sages of India, learning from them to endure discomfort and exposure with indifference. He cultivated an enigmatic persona, traveling incognito even to Athens while Socrates himself was still at large. "I came to Athens and nobody knew me," he almost boasted. Even for a philosopher, Democritus was evasive and coy, his ideas unsettling and counterintuitive.[5]

What he had to teach was that life is an illusion. In sly and cryptic whispers, Democritus insinuated to those in his confidence that most human experience is a passing phantom, a construct of the mind. "The surface of things is a matter of convention," he teased. "It is by convention that things are sweet or bitter."[6] "Convention," *nomos* in Greek, meant a human creation—not a natural feature of the real world, but a system stamped onto the bare material of existence. It was the word for the various legal systems crafted by governing authorities and imposed on the spontaneous rhythms of life, as well as for the

---

4   See Herodotus, *Histories*, 1.168, 7.120.
5   Diogenes Laertius, *Lives of the Eminent Philosophers* 9.35–7.
6   See Democritus, *Fragments* 9 and 49, in Galen, *On the Elements according to Hippocrates* I.2 and Sextus Empiricus, *Adversus Mathematicos* 7.135. Cf. *Hypotheses of Pyrrhonism* I.213–14, Diogenes Laertius, *Lives of Eminent Philosophers* 9.343–45.

artificial scales and melodies used to segment and arrange the natural pitches of sound. *Nomos* meant a formal network layered by humans onto nature.

Democritus suggested that taste and touch are *nomos*, too: we generate them. They come from us. The qualities we experience through our senses—the color of grass or the timbre of birdsong, say—are not real features of the world. They are fabrications, overlaid onto reality by human consciousness, generated by us and dependent on us for existence. Underneath them, things look very different. Beneath the glimmering surface of the world as seen through human eyes, something eerie and alien waits to be discovered.

What lies beneath, what *really* exists, is matter and emptiness. To Democritus, *to kenon* and *sōmata*—an infinite void of space and the bodies within it—were the sum total of everything truly real. That is how Leucippus of Elea put it, and Leucippus seems to have been one of the few masters whose teaching Democritus could accept. "The root components of everything are atoms and void," wrote the third-century AD biographer Diogenes Laertius, explaining Democritus's point of view; "everything else is mere thought."[7] The Greek of Democritus and Leucippus is where we eventually get our own word *atom*—from *atomos*—meaning literally "the uncuttable thing." But whereas our modern atoms have proven troublesomely divisible, in ancient philosophy the atom was by definition the smallest possible object, a solid bead of pure existence.

What Democritus had in mind was perhaps something closer to our notion of a lepton or a quark, if indeed those subatomic

---

7 Diogenes Laertius, *Lives of the Eminent Philosophers* 9.30, 44.

particles are as fundamental as they seem. The point was that somewhere at the basis of all things there must be an object so concrete that it could never be annihilated or deconstructed. Atoms for Democritus were the rawest of raw material. They were simplicity itself: colorless, odorless, stripped of every quality that might be subject to the vagaries of human perception. They would never change shape or number, thought Democritus; they could be neither created nor destroyed. Their quantities, geometric arrangements, and positions in space were appealingly mathematical and so absolutely rational. Wave away the mist of human perception, the clouds of light and noise, and you would arrive at a landscape of crystalline geometrical exactitude across which atoms moved with razorlike precision. Through them, everything could be understood.

Atoms were the base units of everything else, swirling and locking together to produce every object and experience known to man. The taste of sweet food, for example, might be explained as an effect of smooth-shaped atoms caressing the tongue, while the atoms that made up bitter food might prick the mouth with invisibly tiny barbs. The flavor itself would fade in a matter of instants; the food, too, would soon be churned and sluiced through the digestive tract. Every merely human aspect of the experience would start slipping away into the bloodstream or the dirt almost as soon as it began. But underneath it all the atoms would remain, undisturbed and unyielding in their courses, governed by the immutable laws of nature. They endured forever, and they alone were real. So Democritus proposed.

Within a few generations, men came to call him "the laughing philosopher." This was by contrast with Heraclitus of Ephesus, who observed morosely that all things were forever passing away.[8] But this very same notion seemed to Democritus like an occasion for *euthymia*, carefree good cheer: what, me worry? Surely not, when joy and sorrow alike are mere vapors, floating by and vanishing on the surface of the atomic flow like faces in the smoke wafting from a campfire. Early modern paintings of Democritus portray him as variously cackling with wild abandon or curling his lips into a knowing smirk. There was something at once impish and sinister about his invitation to dissolve the world, to laugh into the void. Democritus had stood naked in the temples of India; he had stared across the borders of the Thracian wilderness; he had bared his body and mind to the broad world and found it infinitely unconcerned. The atoms would go on churning and colliding forever—he had no power to alter their outlines by so much as a micrometer. There was nothing to do but smile.

This was not an attitude likely to curry favor with the wealthy scions of mainland Greece. They were striding their way through an invigorating and treacherous era. The High Classical Period was inaugurated by a rousing victory against Persia in 480 BC, and it flamed out shortly thereafter in a disastrous breakdown of relations between the two major powers, Sparta and Athens. Democritus's ideas could hardly catch on amid all the drama and endeavor: this was not the time for meditations on the pointlessness of life or for existentialism *avant la lettre*. Besides, the heartland of philosophy at the time was Athens, and Athenian thought was fixating ever more rigorously on the *purpose* of things. The tradition that began with Socrates and led to Aristotle was

---

8   See for example Cicero, *De Oratore* 2.58.235, Horace, *Epistles* 2.1.194–200, Stobaeus 3.20.53, Juvenal 4.10.28–35, *Letters of pseudo-Hippocrates* 10–21.

increasingly devoted to explanations that could account for the universe as a *kosmos*, an ordered whole. Democritus had little to offer in that regard, since the only order governing his sprawling universe was an impartial set of physical laws. Nor was Aristotle sold on atomistic reasoning: if qualities like "sweet" and "bitter" were just subjective human ideas, he pointed out, it hardly made sense to explain them with reference to "smooth" and "sharp" atoms. The whole system was too arbitrary and disjointed to endure rigorous scrutiny.[9]

But as time wore on, "arbitrary" and "disjointed" would come to seem like fitting descriptions of human life itself. After Athens's abasement at Sparta's hands in the Peloponnesian war (431–404 BC), the Greek-speaking world was left in tatters. The leaders of that world had for a brief moment been engaged in building an ordered latticework of state hierarchies and diplomatic relations. Now this structure buckled abruptly, leaving behind a confusion of rival city-states and shifting allegiances. Alexander the Great's swift rise to power briefly restored unity, of a sort. But it was the forced unity imposed by conquest, and it collapsed immediately after his death in 323 BC. Perhaps this is why the subsequent Hellenistic Era, with its splintered political landscape and its ever-pliable borders, also generated a profusion of philosophical schools. Each one had its own distinctive attitudes and eventually its own internal schisms; each one disputed at least some of the others' claims with vehement intensity. It was a time of contention and disunity, a time of deconstruction and disarray. The perfect time to give Democritus's ideas a second look.

---

9   See further Aristotle, *On Generation and Corruption* I.8 (325a–6a).

The man to do it was Epicurus. He came from Samos off the western coast of Asia Minor. It was a sizeable and glamorous island, its hills draped luxuriously with vineyards; Epicurus was among its chattering classes, the child of Athenian settlers. He himself made his way to Athens in 323 BC, the year Alexander died, and unlike Democritus he was happy to see and be seen. Diogenes Laertius, who was fiercely partial to Epicurus, portrayed him as a high society gentleman dogged unjustly by salacious rumors. Allegedly he gorged himself to the point of vomiting twice a day, leering over courtesans and griping spitefully about his fellow philosophers. All deranged nonsense, insisted Diogenes, but obviously the perception of Epicurus as a reckless hedonist endured to tarnish his reputation long after his death.[10]

To this day, we still use the word *epicurean* to mean "gourmand." If we think of a "stoic" as someone who keeps his passions carefully guarded, then an "epicure" is someone who lines up outside overrated pop-up cafés and drones on about trends in molecular gastronomy as if they carried the significance of the Normandy landings. Epicurus *may* have frittered away his time on self-serious indulgences—the conflicting testimonies surrounding him are too loaded and polemical for us to be sure—but that was definitely not the lifestyle he commended to his students. Unlike the modern meaning of "stoic," the contemporary idea of "epicureanism" bears only the most distant relation to the principles taught expressly in the corresponding ancient school. Hedonism may be a distant consequence of taking Epicurus's advice to heart, but it is not what Epicurus was *about*.

---

10 Diogenes Laertius, 10.3–12.

What he was really up to was spinning out the materialist physics of men like Democritus and Leucippus into a full-fledged scheme of thought and action. To qualify as a complete philosophical system, an ancient doctrine needed to furnish a detailed and internally consistent set of beliefs in three key areas: logic, physics, and ethics. Physics told you what the world was like; logic told you how it could be soundly known; ethics told you what you should do about it. To put it somewhat more precisely: *Logikē*, the study of reason or *logos*, was about how to draw accurate and reliable connections between observations and ideas. *Physikē*, from which we get our word *physics*, covered everything that could be counted as *physis*, "nature": these were the laws and patterns that governed (at least) all material existence. *Ēthikē* dictated how to shape the *ēthos*—the habits and attitudes that make up human character. Since this inevitably involved a theory of what humans are and how they make choices, it was also a study of the *psychē*, the mind or soul. So ethics always involved what we would now call psychology, as well as morality.

Epicurus put forward a countercultural and rigorously materialist set of views in all three areas. Diogenes transcribes the full text of three letters Epicurus wrote to students and followers. He calls them *epitomai*, "epitomes" or condensed summaries of the ideas he worked out more extensively in his books (all of which are lost to us). The letters are intended for general circulation, like handy CliffsNotes for the busy professional. But Epicurus repeatedly stresses that they can serve as memory aids for more advanced students as well, since "it's still quite necessary to refer back to a point-for-point outline of the entire subject and get a reminder of the shape of the thing" (D.L. 10.35–6). Together these letters cover all three of the major topics, though each letter is not devoted exclusively to one subject. The letter to Herodotus (not the historian but a contemporary of Epicurus) begins with basic logic and then uses its methods to outline some principles of physics based on atoms and the void. The letter to Pythocles zooms out from microscopic to macroscopic physics, charting out a theory of weather patterns and celestial movements (favorite subjects of speculation for ancient as well as modern observers). And the letter to Menoeceus outlines a self-help course for living the Epicurean life.

The end goal of that life is pleasure (*hēdonē*), though avowedly *not* the wildly extravagant binge of sex, food, and drugs that we might associate with the word *hedonism*. Those who come to Epicurus seeking license to pass out guilt-free at 3 a.m. in a night-club bathroom will find him no fun at all. He insists (D.L. 10.127–32) that excess and immoderation are actually *obstacles* to a sustainably good life of refined pleasure, which feels less like a cocaine high and more like *ataraxia*. This Greek word is often translated as "peace of mind"; it literally means "not being troubled," and when wielded by Epicurus it suggests a state of blissful enlightenment that modern influencers and life hackers might call "inner peace." The Epicurean's idea of heaven on earth is a place called the "garden," modeled after the cultivated grove where Epicurus would meet with his students, but standing in across time more generally for a kind of "great good place." It is a genteel enclave where men and women alike share in the exquisite delights of good health and philosophy. Its modern analogue is not Jeffrey Epstein's island of sinister debauchery but a selective wellness retreat in the Andes where start-up founders attend seminars on ayurvedic meditation and microdose nootropics. Serenity, not gluttony, is the goal.

The path toward it begins, for Epicurus, with clearing your mind. His idea of logic starts with getting absolutely clear and specific about the meaning of words. "First of all," he writes, "it's crucial to grasp what is designated by the relevant terms, so that by referring to them we can evaluate the ideas being proposed" (D.L. 10.37–38). This welcome admonition brings with it an implicitly favorable comparison to the jargon and hand-waving that accompanies more abstruse forms of philosophy. Clear language means clear thought, and Epicurus wants his language to be ruthlessly exact. He is determined that the superstitions which typically haunt the public, and the high-flown abstractions which philosophers favor, should never creep into his students' minds. This is an invitation to realism: precise language, Epicurus hopes, will keep the discussion to what can be firmly and securely known.

What can be *most* clearly known, at least by us, is *empeiria*: the immediate and direct experience of our own observations. This doesn't mean we're always right about what we see: just because I see water in the desert doesn't mean it's there. But it definitely *does* mean that I'm having the experience of seeing a silvery-blue patch up ahead, and since I can be sure of that experience, I can feel confident about using it as a starting point for further inference. That kind of starting point is what Greek philosophers called a *kritērion*, which is where we get our word *criterion*: It means a "touchstone" of truth, an unshakable fact to test propositions against. The *ideas* that I attach to my experience are another matter: if I have the experience of seeing a blue patch in the desert, I might think, "there's water up ahead." But I may or may not be right: finding out will require further observation and maybe even experiment. Epicurus was a precursor not only to philosophers like David Hume and Francis Bacon, who insisted on direct experience as the basis for reasoning and science, but also to René Descartes, who knew he existed because he could think, and something had to be doing the thinking. Epicurus knew that sense experiences existed, because he was having them.

Other things exist too, but knowing about them depends on the devilishly tricky business of moving from sense experience to unperceived or imperceptible things (D.L. 10.38–40). For Epicurus this means reasoning from what is manifest (*to dēlon*) to what is not or cannot be seen (*to adēlon*). A treacherous journey—but it has to be attempted, because one of the things that cannot be seen is the atom, and that is the most real thing of all. There is an interesting paradox here, one that has bedeviled atomists and empiricists ever since. On the one hand, sense perception is the only firm and reliable source of knowledge about reality. On the other hand, the most fundamental aspect of reality, the atom, cannot be registered by sense perception! Epicurus goes so far as to says that we cannot even *conceive* of atoms big enough to be seen (D.L. 10.56). So how do we know they're there?

Epicurus's answer, and ours, is that we know about atoms indirectly, by observing the impact they make on our senses or our measuring devices. The shifting fog of experience and sensation that wafts around us is just a product of the interaction between the atoms outside of us and the atoms in our bodies. Qualities like color and smell are "known by the senses themselves" and "cannot be thought of as existing by nature in themselves." Instead they are kicked up by the same blind swirling of atoms that spontaneously created our own bodies and souls (which are also made of atoms).

Atoms themselves, by contrast, are just bare matter, unencumbered by frivolous phantoms of the mind like texture or sound. They "have no qualities such as belong to perceptible phenomena, except for shape, weight, magnitude, and whatever else necessarily pertains to the nature of shape," writes Epicurus (D.L. 10.54). He sounds exactly like Descartes: "The nature of matter or body in its universal aspect does not consist in its being hard, or heavy, or colored, or anything that affects our senses in any other way, but solely in the fact that it is a substance extended in length, breadth, and depth."[11] But what on earth gives us license to attribute those properties to atoms, which we cannot see, while discarding as mere human constructs all the other forms and shades of things, which we do see?

We can tabulate and measure the motion of bodies through space, which we cannot do to a memory or the color of gold. But the source of those measurements, just like the source of memories and the sensation of beauty, is in our experience. We will never touch or see an atom in its supposedly "pure" form, stripped of every visible or tangible property—what would it even mean to see something with no color, or hear something that is not a sound? All we can do is observe the impact of objects on our senses, or look at data readouts from a hadron collider, and *infer* facts about the unseeable particles we think caused those experiences. But the mind that looks at numbers on a screen and interprets them is the same mind that translates the tremors of the air into the sound of thunder. The Epicurean insistence—that the tremors are somehow more real than the sound—starts to feel less like scientific rigor and more like

---

11 Descartes, *Principia Philosophiae* II.4. See further *The World*, chapter 6.

motivated reasoning based on materialist prejudice. Experience cannot show us that only bodies exist; if anything, our predetermined belief that only bodies exist is what *teaches* us to affirm certain experiences and discount others. But if our experience is the foundation of all our knowledge, why does only measurable experience count as real?

Epicurus never leans too hard on this question. It is the weakest point of his theory. It is also the root of everything else. For stripping down the world to its atomic components is what justifies Epicurus in claiming that the highest good of life is serenity in the here and now. His physics is the source of his ethics. Like Democritus before him, he views human life as a happy accident produced by slow evolutionary degrees in the natural course of atomic flow—and this, he thinks, is reason to enjoy the brief flirtation of matter with consciousness while it lasts. When our bodies stop working, the supple atoms that communicate sensation to our flesh will slip away again like mist, and with that our souls will evaporate back into the atmosphere. The gods—perfect beings of pure serenity, whose atomic composition is presumably far more durable and stable than ours—did not make the world, or us. They are not waiting to punish or reward us after death. There will be no "us" to punish or reward: when the atoms of the body dissolve, so does the self (D.L. 10.123–6).

It follows that the bliss of the present moment is the point of life—if life can be said to have a point. The only reason Epicurus *doesn't* advise orgiastic self-indulgence is because he doesn't think that's the most pleasant way to live. "The virtues and the life of pleasure are twins from birth, and pleasurable living is inseparable from the virtues" (D.L. 132). But we know virtue is good *because* it makes our lives more enjoyable while they last, not the other way around: the pleasure, not the virtue, is the point (D.L. 127–131). This is a daring inversion of classical ethics, but in most cases it turns out to be more of an academic hypothetical than a consequential distinction. Like utilitarians and evolutionary psychologists after him, Epicurus could always come up with some reason why the conventional virtues really are the ones that make our lives most satisfying—in fact, he indicates, that is why we aspire to them in the first place.

A life of moderation, generosity, and honor—a life spent cultivating friendship and calming the mind through philosophy—really is the most enjoyable kind of life, argues Epicurus. If some other kind of life were more enjoyable, we would choose it. But that lingering counterfactual is exactly where the system breaks down. One wonders what happens in the labor camps and the hospital ward—when courage and sacrifice mean suffering followed by a death which, according to Epicurus, snuffs out the flame of the mind forever. No purely naturalist or evolutionary account can explain why the father might go to the gas chambers in place of his son—no Epicurean argument can underwrite nobility like that. It takes some reality bigger than atoms, and some purpose higher than pleasure, to bring out the best in the human soul.

• • •

The translations in this volume are my own originals. I have included all three letters of Epicurus in full, plus selections from the poem *De Rerum Natura*, "On the Nature of Things." This is a six-book epic written during the turbulent dying years of the Roman Republic by Titus Lucretius Carus, usually referred to simply as Lucretius. The poem is addressed to Gaius Memmius, a politician and a man of letters, but it is designed to sell the Roman gentry more broadly on Epicureanism, in which Lucretius firmly believes. He is fighting an uphill battle, as he well knows: it would be a tall order to translate the elaborate technicalities of *any* Greek philosophy into Latin hexameters (the meter of glorious war epics and grand adventure stories). And Epicureanism was likely to be a particularly tough sell. But Lucretius executes his task ably; the result is a virtuosic tour de force and a master class in making philosophy vivid. It is one of the great works of Latin literature in its own right, and our only source for much of what we know about Epicureanism. Readers who want the whole thing can go to Martin Ferguson Smith's translation (Indianapolis: Hackett, 1969) or Rolfe Humpries (Bloomington, IN: Indiana University Press, 1969), and for the full Diogenes (including more on Epicurus) there is a fantastic new edition translated by Pamela Mensch (Oxford: Oxford University Press, 2018). Both authors are also available in bilingual editions from Harvard University's Loeb Classical Library series.

Other sources on Epicureanism which survive in fragments—like the inscription by Diogenes of Oenoanda found on a battered wall in Turkey, or the polemical surveys by Philodemus of Gadara—are probably beyond the interest of the general reader, at least for now. Philodemus was part of a limited but influential circle of Roman elites (among whom Virgil seems to have moved). The ash of Vesuvius buried the house of Philodemus's benefactor, the senator Lucius Calpurnius Piso, tantalizingly preserving his personal library in a fragile and damaged state. Scholars have been picking over the charred remains of those scrolls for centuries, but even as I was writing this book a stunning breakthrough in machine-learning technology made it possible to read far more of them than ever before.[12] It's not sensationalist to imagine that genuine revelations about ancient history—including Roman Epicureanism—will emerge in the next few years. Still, Lucretius's poem remains the core source, and I've picked out some passages here that will flesh out ideas which Epicurus only touches on or doesn't even mention—like the invisibility of atoms, or the "swerve" in atomic motion that makes free will possible.[13] Finally, though, I've also done something a little unconventional for a collection like this: I've included a few passages and selections from the modern world, especially the dawn of the scientific revolution.

Because that is when Epicureanism was reborn. Like Epicurus in the Hellenistic Era, the first practitioners of modern science came of age during a period of traumatic international breakdown. Doubts that had begun to fester during the late Medieval era were hypercharged by the printing press. The seemingly immovable cosmic structure of truth and order, underwritten by Church authority, began to totter. Finally it collapsed in on itself with the calamitous bloodbath of the Thirty Years' War (1618–1648). The bruised nations of Europe would never agree on a shared faith again, which meant that the world was left without an overriding arbiter who could unfold the mysteries of the world and judge competing claims to truth. The inheritors of the wreckage had to wonder: what can possibly be known, and how? It was

---

12 See Jo Marchant, "First Passages of Rolled-Up Herculaneum Scroll Revealed," in *Nature*, February 2024. https://www.nature.com/articles/d41586–024 -00346–8.

13 If Epicurus did believe in the swerve (he doesn't mention it anywhere, but Lucretius reports it as one of his beliefs) this was a rare departure from the views of Democritus.

in that moment that Epicurus's answer recommended itself again: the solid facts of the material world, tangible and sturdy as the ground itself, could be relied upon. That was the beginning of the revolution.

Schoolchildren who study the roots of modern science typically hear a tidy story about new methods and their exciting results. It usually features men like Galileo Galilei, Isaac Newton, and Francis Bacon learning to hone their hypotheses and experiments until they can isolate the causes and effects that make apples fall and planets spin. Maybe for a touch of spice there are a few morality tales about "religious opposition" in the form of one or two isolated vignettes plucked selectively from Galileo's lengthy battle of wills with Cardinal Robert Bellarmine and the papal authorities. At the end of this neat little chronicle there ensues a glorious transition from darkness into light: the forces of superstition and ignorance are overthrown, clearing the way for more rational and liberated attitudes. These in turn eventually deliver the wondrous technologies we enjoy today.

But astonishing though those technologies indeed are, it takes more than gadgets to transform the world. The trailblazing innovators of the seventeenth and eighteenth centuries were not just devising new procedures for laboratory research, though they were certainly doing that. Nor were they proposing to overthrow religion, whatever that might have meant. Most of them were themselves believers of some variety or another, arguing with fellow believers about the best way to understand creation. And *within* that argument they were putting forward a particular way of looking at and relating to the world. But their success was so shocking and so total that it did ultimately upend everything—including religious belief. It was an upheaval in philosophy that would not only generate new protocols for studying nature, but also shatter the foundational assumptions of the public at large. In time, new assumptions would take hold, reorienting the average person in relation to his surroundings and his fellow man. In the modern as in the ancient world, physics never leaves ethics untouched.

The ideas about physics that eventually won out were alarming and unusual for their time, but they were not altogether new. Direct experience is the source of all certain knowledge about the natural world, which is made of quantifiable *stuff*, or matter: that idea, or some version of it, was the lodestar of early modern innovators. They took it directly from Epicurus. Some of them said so explicitly. David Hume, one of the first to become an out-and-out atheist, put the most controversial chapter of his *Enquiry Concerning Human Understanding* into the mouth of Epicurus. In it, he argued that no one who looked honestly at the ramshackle construction of the physical universe had any rational grounds for concluding that it was the product of supreme intelligence or care. "This superlative intelligence and benevolence are entirely imaginary, or, at least, without any foundation in reason," says Hume's Epicurus: nature goes shuddering along without perfect divine oversight (XI.106). Thousands of years before, Lucretius had already summarized Epicurus in much the same way: "Spontaneous, she does the things she does," he wrote of nature. "She knows no gods" (2.1090–92).

Not all the new philosophers were as skeptical as Hume. But they agreed that certain knowledge was less likely to come from speculating about spiritual abstractions than from studying objects, reassuringly tangible and measurable as they are supposed to be. This too was an Epicurean impulse, and it led back to that curious Epicurean paradox: We know about matter through our senses, by

seeing and experiencing it. But matter itself, in its essence, is supposedly *not* the way we experience it: it has no color, or smell, or
texture. Those, thought the new Epicureans, are just human fan-
cies, arbitrary constructs that the mind devises to clothe the pure
and featureless essence of pure matter. This was an idea that already
started resurfacing in the days of Galileo: "I think that tastes, odors,
colors, and so on are no more than mere names so far as the object
in which we place them is concerned, and that they reside only in
the consciousness," he wrote.[14] The face of Democritus was looming
over the landscape again, grinning that old Cheshire Cat grin.

The division was between "primary qualities"—measurable
and objective properties like number and weight—and "secondary
qualities"—subjective human experiences like color and sound.
This thoroughly Epicurean distinction now stuck deep into the
public consciousness like a chasm between mind and heart. On
one side was everything that could be measured and weighed,
counted and graphed. On the other side was pure illusion: color
and form, memory and desire, deceit and dreams. "That is real
which can be measured"—this, according to Martin Heidegger,
was the conviction of the 20th-century physicist Max Planck.[15]
Reaching out in the fractured ruins for something solid to build
with, the architects of the new world grasped on to numbers and
matter. Those alone, they thought, could be counted on as real.

---

14 Galileo Galilei, *The Assayer*. See *The Essential Galileo*, ed. and trans. Maurice
    A. Finocchiaro (Indianapolis, IN: Hackett, 2008), 179–89. Cf. Owen Barfield,
    Worlds Apart: A Dialogue of the 1960's [sic], first published 1963 (Oxford:
    Barfield Press, 2010), 93–96.
15 Martin Heidegger, "Science and Reflection," in *The Question Concerning
    Technology and Other* Essays, trans. William Lovitt. (New York: Harper
    Torchbooks, 1977), 169.

Any number system needs a base unit, and so the return of Epicureanism also meant the return of the atom—not just the word but the faith in small particles, the belief that somewhere at the bedrock of things there were grains of indivisible matter that could serve as the foundation stones of the world. "We have the whole course of a large experience for the universal gravity of matter and for the hardness of its particles without any instance to the contrary," wrote Newton, venturing a guess that material reality, when pared down to its essentials, was made of solid particles.[16] In some sense it *had* to be, though by their nature these component parts of existence could never be experienced directly. It wasn't just that they were too small: it was that they were too pure, stripped of all the secondary qualities that frail human perception needed in order to experience things.

If it is a random product of the mechanical universe, the human mind can hardly hope to know the essence of existence directly. The irony is that believing only in matter, because you can see and touch it, leads to believing that matter in its essence cannot be seen or touched. If the core of reality is a world indifferent to our minds and inaccessible to our senses, we can never hope to know anything about it. Yet the faith of Epicureans old and new has always been that atoms *do*, in fact, go on colliding and combining, eternally and unchangingly, by the laws of nature. As the scientific age wore on, that faith became almost messianic. Bacon already saw in the atom a material replacement for the love that was thought to have made the world: "This Love I understand to be the appetite or instinct of primal matter; or to speak more plainly, *the natural motion of the*

---

16 Newton, 1716 draft of projected addition to *Opticks* III. See further *Opticks* Query 31 and Ernan McMullin, *Newton on Matter and Activity* (Notre Dame, IN: University of Notre Dame Press, 1978), 143 n. 128.

atom; which is indeed the original and unique force that constitutes and fashions all things out of matter."[17] James Clerk Maxwell, pioneer of electromagnetism, reaffirmed the creed in 1873: "though in the course of ages catastrophes have occurred and may yet occur in the heavens, though ancient systems may be dissolved and new systems evolved out of their ruins, the molecules out of which these systems are built—the foundation stones of the material universe—remain unbroken and unworn."[18]

In this world, at least, atoms alone are eternal and objects alone are real: that is the Epicurean statement of faith. This time around, it has not remained limited to an exclusive caste of initiates and their favored clerisy. The new Epicureanism has become a governing public conviction, an unseen operating system that informs our most widespread assumptions. It reaches from the highest halls of power and knowledge to the studios and boardrooms where commercial entertainment is produced. "All things are made of atoms," said the physicist Richard Feynman to freshman classes at CalTech. This was, he thought, the idea from which all other scientific knowledge could be built: atoms are "little particles that move around in perpetual motion, attracting each other when they are a little distance apart, but repelling upon being squeezed into one another."[19] In its more popular iterations, atomic theory is not just a mathematical model but a source of

---

17 Bacon, *Of the Wisdom of the Ancients* XVII: "Cupid, or The Atom," in *The Works of Francis Bacon: Literary and Professional Works*, ed. James Spedding, Robert Leslie Ellis, and Douglas Denon Heath (Cambridge: Cambridge University Press, 2013), vol. 6.

18 James Clerk Maxwell, "Molecules," *Nature* 8 (1873): 437–441, 441.

19 Richard Feynman, *The Feynman Lectures on Physics*, ed. Michael A. Gottlieb and Rudolph Pfeiffer (Pasadena: The California Institute of Technology, 1961), Vol. 1, Ch. 1. https://www.feynmanlectures.caltech.edu.

conventional wisdom. "We're all just made of molecules and we're hurtling through space right now," said comedian Sarah Silverman in an acceptance speech at the Emmys. In the routine for which she won the award, Silverman proclaimed: "[T]here was a time in history, a blip ago in the scope of history, where we were all microscopic specks."[20]

And if everything is atoms, then pleasure is the highest good. It is no accident that "wellness," "safety," and "serenity" have become subjects of near obsession in the new Age of Epicurus. These are modern forms of *ataraxia*. Pursuing them is the point of life, if life is just the transient consequence of a temporary atomic configuration, soon to be dissolved. "There is no me," says a dying woman at the end of writer-director Mike Flanagan's Netflix series *Midnight Mass*. "There never was. The electrons of my body mingle and dance with the electrons of the ground below me and the air I'm no longer breathing."[21] The summit of insight is to learn that "death is nothing to us," so life is merely about maximizing utility and minimizing harm in the short space between birth and death. In the meantime we seek experiences that are, in the words of one infamous sexologist, "safe, fulfilling, and pleasurable."[22]

20 Sarah Silverman, *We Are Miracles*. HBO, 2014. https://www.youtube.com /watch?v=xSiM5v-S_eY; "Sarah Silverman Wins for Writing for a Variety Special." Television Academy. https://www.youtube.com/watch?v=v246gNqIfTU.

21 "Revelation," *Midnight Mass* Season 1, episode 7, dir. Mike Flanagan. Netflix: September 24, 2021.

22 See Melissa Koenig, "'People are Aroused by Electrocution,'" *Daily Mail*, June 4, 2021. https://www.dailymail.co.uk/news/article-9650967/Leaked-porn -lecture-given-Manhattan-school-reveals-pupils-taught-electro-porn.html; Valeriya Safronova, "A Private-School Sex Educator Defends Her Methods," *New York Times*, July 7, 2021. https://www.nytimes.com/2021/07/07/style /sex-educator-methods-defense.html.

Having performed this mass experiment in Epicureanism, we can now confirm that it's not excess or indulgence that's the real problem, as Epicurus's own detractors imagined. It's lassitude and hopelessness. As it happens, a life lived on the passing eddy of an infinite atomic river is neither particularly pleasant nor even all that conducive to peace of mind. Surging despair, depression, overmedication, overwhelming unease: these are the metrics of souls crying out for something more than matter to make sense of the world.[23] The eager optimism of the technological age has soured into fears of humanity's total annihilation or replacement by machines—because, of course, if all we are is matter, there's no reason why better, faster, stronger matter shouldn't outstrip us.[24]

---

23 See for example Dan Witters, "U.S. Depression Rates Reach New Highs," *Gallup*, May 17, 2023. https://news.gallup.com/poll/505745/depression-rates -reach-new-highs.aspx; Laura Dattner, "Youth Suicide and Attempted Suicide Reported to Poison Control Centers Increased During the COVID-19 Pandemic," *Pediatrics Nationwide*, April 04, 2023. https://pediatricsnationwide .org/2023/04/04/youth-suicide-and-attempted-suicide-increased-during-the -covid-19-pandemic/. Cf. Hans Jonas, *The Phenomenology of Life: Toward a Philosophical Biology* (Evanston, IL: Northwestern University Press, 1966), 108–34.

24 See further r/antinatalism, a subreddit with 213,000 members as of January 2024: https://www.reddit.com/r/antinatalism/; Rebecca Tuhus-Dubrow; "I Wish I'd Never Been Born: The Rise of the Antinatalists," in *The Guardian*, November 14 2019. https://archive.ph/Yy7FW; David Benatar, *Better Never to Have Been: The Harm of Coming into Existence* (Oxford: Oxford University Press, 2006). Hence Elon Musk frequently argues that "the real battle is between the extinctionists and the humanists." @elonmusk, October 31, 2023. https://x.com/elonmusk/status/1719398881870356695?s=20. See further Cara Buckley, "Earth Now Has 8 Billion Humans. This Man Wishes There Were None," *New York Times*, November 23, 2023. https://www.nytimes.com/2022 /11/23/climate/voluntary-human-extinction.html.

The thought of ourselves as "ape-brained meatsacks," saddled with contemptible misperceptions and weaknesses, has left more than a few people ready to crawl out of their skins in an effort to commune directly with the dispassionate perfection of pure machinery.[25] "We're willing to divorce, open to divorce from ourselves all human norms, all human customs, all human thought," announced techno-futurist Bryan Johnson, describing what he considers the first generation to leap into the inevitable post-human future.[26] In an Epicurean universe, our options are to accept the futility and limitations of human life, or somehow repudiate our humanity altogether. Neither option particularly inspires delight. It turns out that atoms alone won't cut it: Epicurean materialism fails to set the mind at rest as its evangelists promise it will. All it really does is leave us flailing in a riptide of atomic flow, desperate not to melt back into the ocean. Desperate for something more than death, and then nothing.

Good news, then, that the Epicurean ideas of the scientific revolution have been falling to pieces for more than a hundred years. Our conventional wisdom and our pop psychology have yet to take stock of the fact that classical physics, useful as it is, does not describe the final and absolute reality of things. The world of solid atoms in eternal flux is not the real world; it is only a mathematical picture, a model we can use from time to time to sketch out certain trends in our observations. When we try to get "underneath" those observations to the supposedly hard and pure

25 See Elise Bohan, *Future Superhuman: Our Transhuman Lives in a Make-or-Break Century* (New South Wales: NewSouth Publishing, 2022), 11, 23–25.
26 Bryan Johnson, interview with Rich Roll, "The $2M Longevity Protocol: Bryan Johnson's Biohacking Blueprint," on *The Rich Roll Podcast*, January 29, 2024. https://www.youtube.com/watch?v=roHeUk7ApUo.

material world, we find that there is actually no escaping human experience, no way of slipping free from our own consciousness into a world of pure data and "primary qualities." As quantum physics has been suggesting for some time, and readers of the Book of Genesis have always known, the world comes most fully into being when it is *seen*. The smallest building blocks of the cosmos are less like minute grains of sand than they are like bits of information, starlike pinpricks of knowledge waiting to be known.[27] Human consciousness is not a creature of accident or convention—it is essential. Atoms are not the only component parts of the world. Mind, just as much as matter, makes up reality.

Which means that Epicurus's whole edifice must come tumbling down. What science has been discovering in the years since Max Planck is that consciousness is not so dispensable after all. We are not just piles of atoms on a cold rock. We are the minds that make the universe bear its fruit, the cultivators of creation's garden, the souls in whom reality takes on its full array of color and form. The passages in this book are testaments to a marvelously subtle, and often very useful, system of thought. They describe a way of reasoning that has proven its powers and attractions for many hundreds of years. But in the end, as a system of belief and a way of life, Epicureanism has proven a total failure.

---

27 See esp. John Archibald Wheeler, "Information, Physics, Quantum: The Search for Links," in *Proceedings of the 3rd International Symposium in the Foundations of Quantum Mechanics*, ed. Hiroshi Ezawa, Shun Ichi Kobayashi, and Yoshimasa Murayama (Tokyo: Physics Society of Japan, 1989), 354–68; see further George Musser, *Putting Ourselves Back in the Equation* (New York, Farrar, Straus and Giroux, 2023), 12, 106–7; *Light of the Mind, Light of the World: How New Science is Illuminating Ancient Truths About God*, by Spencer A. Klavan (Washington, DC: Regnery, 2024). Forthcoming.

That failure, too, is well worth reckoning with, because it has afflicted us so totally and for so long. For centuries, we have all been Epicureans. Only once we realize that can we hope to become something more.

PART I

The Letters of Epicurus

The Letter to Herodotus
(Diogenes Laertius 10.34–84)

This letter outlines Epicurus's main principles of logic and physics, arguing that everything is either atoms or void. Modern readers will be interested to find here (and in the next letter) a theory of "many worlds." This is a precursor to multiverse theory, motivated by many of the same concerns: if atoms and the laws of physics explain everything, and if the order of our world is not the product of divine forethought, then many or even all possible worlds must come into being by chance. See further the third passage from Lucretius in this collection.

Epicurus to Herodotus

Greetings,

[35] For those, Herodotus, who can't carefully examine each point that we wrote out in our books on nature, or make a thorough

1

study of the longer books we've written up on the subject, I myself have prepared a summary of the whole subject, designed to provide a summation of all the major points in outline, to help them jog their own memories on the most pertinent points in each of the topics, whenever they should touch on the theory of nature. And even for those who are more advanced in their study of the whole topic, it's still quite necessary to refer back to a point-for-point outline of the entire subject and get a reminder of the shape of the thing. After all, we often need an overview of the whole subject gathered together—less often the parts one by one.

[36] Well then, we have to return constantly to each of the main principles and fix them so firmly in our memory that our approach to the details will be utterly sound. And even the finer points will all be clearly elucidated as part of the whole once we have grasped the shape of the thing overall and memorized its outline, since even for a highly accomplished student the most reliable source of clarity in every particular is to be able to refer precisely to first principles so as to relate each issue to its arrangement in the whole and apply the appropriate terminology. For no one can take in the full view of all the parts gathered into an orderly array unless he can sum up with the whole thing in itself and express with simple words what could be divided up into parts.

[37] In view of which, since this approach is helpful for all those engaging with the study of nature, and since I myself pursue that study with diligence and enthusiasm—having attained serenity through this kind of pursuit, more than any other—I've made for you just such a summary and outline of all the main ideas.

First of all, then, Herodotus, it's crucial to grasp what is designated by the relevant terms, so that by referring to them we can evaluate the ideas being proposed, or examined, or called into doubt, and so as not to be drawn into redundant demonstrations ad infinitum or saddled with meaningless terms. [38] It's essential that the primary ideas we work with should each be known by simple terms requiring no further demonstration, which is how we will get a reference point to which we can refer whatever is being examined, or doubted, or proposed.

Next, it's necessary to scrutinize thoroughly our sensory experiences, and all our present impressions more generally, whether in the mind or from some other source of knowledge—and likewise all existing feelings, so we have a means of drawing inferences about what is not evident and what has yet to be confirmed.

Proceeding in this manner, we need next to take stock of the principles concerning what is not evident. First, nothing comes out of what doesn't exist. For if no sources were necessary to produce things, anything could arise out of anything. [39] And if anything were to disappear and be consumed by nonexistence, all things whatsoever would be destroyed, since they would be resolved into component parts that do not exist. Indeed, the sum total of all things was always the same as it is now, and it will always be the same. For there is nothing into which it can change. Besides the sum total there is nothing, so it can't transition into anything to make a change.

Moreover, [and he says this also near the beginning of the *Larger Survey* and in his book *On Nature*],[1] the sum total is bodies

---

1 Diogenes occasionally interjects to comment or cross-reference sections of the letters with other works and statements by Epicurus as he understands them. It is usually clear where he picks up and leaves off, but in some edge cases editors have to use their judgment. I have indicated the passages where I believe Diogenes intervenes by enclosing them in square brackets.

and empty space. Sense perception itself bears witness to the existence of bodies. By these same means we are compelled to reason about what is not evident using sensory indicators. [40] If there did not exist that other aspect of nature, which we designate by the names "emptiness" and "vacuum" and "intangible," then bodies would have no place through which to move. But they do appear to move. Besides these two things, nothing can be conceived, either by cognition or something analogous to cognition—that is, when bodies and emptiness are grasped as essential natures in themselves, rather than spoken of as aspects or inessential features of something else.

Among bodies, then [and he says this in the first book of *On Nature* as well as in the fourteenth and fifteenth of the *Larger Survey*], some are compounds, and others are what the compounds are made out of—that is to say, [41] they are indivisible and unchangeable elements. Otherwise all things would be doomed to dissolve into nonexistence. Instead the elements endure securely throughout the decomposition of compounds, since they are solid by nature and have no place or way to be dissolved. The result is that all primary entities must necessarily be indivisible bodies by nature.

Moreover, the sum total of all things is infinite. For what is finite has a limit, and the limit is discerned by comparison to something else. Where there is no limit, there is no "beyond"; so the sum total of things, having no beyond, is limitless and infinite.

Next, the sum total of things is infinite in the quantity of its bodies and in the volume of its empty space. [42] For if the void were infinite, but the bodies were of finite number, the bodies would not stay in one place but be carried around and scattered through the infinite emptiness, with no one and nothing to oversee or arrange them by any manner of restraint. And if the emptiness were circumscribed, the infinite bodies would have no space to occupy and nowhere to be.

It may be added that those bodies which are indivisible and solid, the "atoms" from which compounds are made and into which they are dissolved, are inconceivably varied in their shapes: it is not possible that so much variety could have been formed out of the same shapes. And for each shape there is a completely limitless number of bodies with the identical shape, though the number of types of shape is not completely unlimited—only impossible to conceive [43] [for he says later that they are not infinitely divided, adding "since the qualities change"]—unless one intends to multiply their masses infinitely.

And the atoms are in perpetual, continuous motion [he says below that they also move with equal speed, since the empty space gives way to the weightiest and the lightest of them equally]. Some are separated from each other by a great distance, whereas others vibrate in place whenever they find themselves locked in a bond or entangled and subsumed into other bonded structures.

[44] The conditions for these interactions are furnished by the nature of empty space, which separates each atom individually and cannot provide it with any resistance. And the solidity which is inherent in the atoms causes them to rebound upon collision, whether for a short or long distance, and find themselves bound in a compound again. These motions have no beginning, since both atoms and void are everlasting. [He says below that the atoms exhibit no qualities except for shape, size, and weight, arguing in *The Twelve Basic Principles* that color is a result of the

atoms' changing arrangement. And he says that they are not of every size: at least, no atom has ever been detected by direct sense perception.]

[45] Once these terms are repeated at length and committed to memory, they will provide, in outline, a sufficient foundation for contemplating all existing entities in nature.

Now, worlds are also limitless—some of them are like this one, others are unlike. For the atoms are limitless, as was just demonstrated, and they are continually being carried further and further. The kinds of atoms necessary to make or give birth to a world are never used up, either in one world or in a limited number of them, whether they are like ours or different. It follows that there is nothing to prevent an unlimited number of worlds.

[46] And furthermore there are shapes in the same outline as those of solid objects, though they far surpass all perceptible things in thinness. For no such composition is impossible to form in the surrounding space, nor are the conditions unsuitable for the creation of thin and hollow emanations, which flow forth and maintain the same strictly ordered arrangement as the solid atoms have—these emanated shapes are what we call "images." And indeed their trajectory through the void, if they meet with no opposition from any body moving in a different direction, can cover any conceivable distance in an unthinkably short time. For slowness and speed correspond to resistance and its absence.

[47] But in terms of time intervals that can be conceived and discussed in theory, the moving body does not arrive simultaneously at multiple places—that would be inconceivable. But in time as we perceive it, the image is both here and there at once without any delay, even if it is not arriving from the place where we perceive it to be. For delay would amount to resistance, even

if up to this point we allow that its trajectory has met with no resistance. This is, in general, a useful point to bear in mind. The fact that the images possess an unsurpassed thinness is not contradicted by any observed phenomena, from which it follows that they have an unsurpassed speed, since they always have space sufficient to pass through in limitless quantities without hitting up against anything, or only a few things, even where many or even all atoms would bump into something right away.

[48] Next, consider that the creation of the images happens as quickly as thought. For the flow of images from the surface of bodies is continuous and the bodies do not seem to shrink, because the images are immediately replaced, retaining for a long while the arrangement of solid objects and the order they acquired from the atoms—even if sometimes there is a slight confusion. These images are formed quickly in the surrounding air, because they do not need to maintain the density of solid bodies. And certain other conditions are productive of similar effects. After all, nothing in our perceived experience contradicts these claims, if one considers the vivid impressions and experiences that are conferred upon us from outside of ourselves.

[49] We must also conclude that we see and consider things when something comes into us from outside. For our surroundings would not impress the contours, colors, and forms of their own constitution upon us through the air between us and them, nor through rays of light or some kind of fluid coming out of us to them, but rather from certain shapes coming into our sight or thought from the things outside of us, in such a way as to retain the same colors and forms in the appropriate proportions, making swift use of the necessary pathways, [50] and then furnishing by this means an appearance of one unitary and consistent thing,

retaining all the interconnections of the atoms in the underlying object by way of a proportional impact according to the density and the vibration of the atoms. Which appearance, if we apprehended it directly in the mind or through the sensory organs either with regard to its form or its incidental attributes, will be the same form as that of the solid object, arising out of the compounding or residue of the images. False claims and contradictions, by contrast, always consist in judgments of assent or dissent added on to perceptions, when they are either not yet confirmed or contradicted by sense impressions [according to a certain motion in us ourselves, associated with the appearance impressing itself upon us, but diverging from it in some way, by which it becomes false].

[51] And the resemblance of such appearances as we experience in artistic depictions or encounter in dreams or other forms of mental apprehension, or from the other sources of impressions, would never resemble truly existent things if there were not some other such thing we had encountered. That is, ideas that are contradicted by experience would not exist if we did not take some foreign motion within that is associated with the appearances that impress themselves upon us, though it diverges from them in some way. And by this means, if our assertion is either not attested by sense impressions or contradicted by them, there is falsehood. If on the other hand it is attested or not contradicted, there is truth.

[52] Indeed, it's of the utmost importance to hold firm in these convictions, so as not to reject sources of truth that are based on manifest evidence, or to let misconceptions, reinforced as if true, cause all manner of disturbance.

So then, hearing also takes place when a stream is carried from some source that is speaking, resonating, booming, or otherwise making noise in some way, and produces a sensation. This stream is distributed among particles of like mass, each of which simultaneously retains an affinity with the others and a unity within itself. Each one has a connection to the original source and so can produce the relevant perception in itself just as well as a multitude, or, failing that, can indicate the external source of the impression. [53] For without some mutual interaction to carry the impression from that source, this form of perception would never occur. Not that it's necessary to think of the air itself being shaped by the voice (or anything else of that nature) as it issues forth—air is not remotely susceptible to that kind of influence. Rather, whenever we produce a sound, an impact made within us instantly produces a corresponding stream of breathy pressure, transmitted through small masses, which produces the sensation of hearing in us. Likewise, odor should be thought of similarly to sound: no impression would ever be formed if external objects did not emit certain masses with the appropriate properties to stimulate the sensory organ—some of them chaotically and disjointedly, others smoothly and pleasingly.

[54] Also, it must be believed that atoms have no qualities such as belong to perceptible phenomena except for shape, weight, magnitude, and whatever else necessarily pertains to the nature of shape. For every quality changes, but the atoms never change in any way, since something solid and indestructible has to stay the same throughout the decomposition of compounds—something that will keep changes from moving into nonexistence or out of it, making them consist instead in the rearrangement of multiple elements, or the addition and subtraction of a few units. Which means that by necessity the things being rearranged must be imperishable and without any shadow of change by nature,

possessing mass and shape simply in themselves. Such things will necessarily endure.

[55] Even among those things that, from our perspective, are taken to change shape by giving off particles, we grasp that the shape endures in the thing that is changing, while the qualities do not, since the shape persists, but the qualities arise out of the whole body and are destroyed with it. So what remains is sufficient to account for differences among the compounds, since something must necessarily be left and not decompose into nothingness.

But no one should be under the impression that atoms can have just any size; if he is he will be directly contradicted by the observable phenomena. We should think of the atoms as exhibiting a limited range of variation in size. This will also produce a better assessment of the evidence our senses provide and the actual impressions we get of what happens.

[56] Imagining just any size at all to exist would not help to explain the actual differences in qualities, and if there were atoms of all sizes then some visible ones would have reached us, which has never been observed—nor is it even possible to conceive of a visible atom coming into existence.

In addition, it should not be imagined that within a limited body it is possible to store unlimited masses, however small. So not only is it unsuitable to imagine infinite division into ever-smaller pieces, so that we do not make everything totally impotent and force existing things into nonexistence by grinding them down into nothing with the way we conceive of compounds, but we also must not imagine that the empty spaces within limited bodies can be subdivided infinitely into smaller and smaller increments.

[57] For there is no way to conceive, if someone should ever claim that some object is comprised of unlimited masses, however small, where that object's dimensions would ever stop. For clearly the unlimited masses would be of some definite size, and whatever size that might be, the overall dimensions would be limitless. It must be granted that limited bodies have boundaries and end-points, even if they cannot be observed. And it is impossible not to conceive of another such object next to that one, and another one next to that, and in this way by continuing to add bodies to each other it is possible to proceed in thought on to infinity.

[58] We should think of the smallest bodies visible to our perception as not altogether the same as those that we can travel across, one region at a time, but not altogether dissimilar either, so that they have certain things in common, except that the smallest bodies have no parts. But when we think that through a kind of resemblance in common between these two types, we can divide the smallest bodies into parts here or there, we must actually be considering another body of equal size. We consider these smallest things one by one, starting with the first, and not occupying the same place or touching one another at any part, but each one serving as a unit of the overall magnitude, which is greater if there are more of them, and smaller if there are fewer.

[59] We will have to think by means of this analogy about what pertains to the atom. For it is clear that it differs from things that can be perceived by the senses in being vastly more minute, but we can consider it by analogy. It was by this analogy that we showed the atom to have size in the first place, projecting small things onto a larger scale. So we must imagine the smallest possible distance as a pure limit of all lengths and a standard by which to measure the larger and smaller atoms, outlining with

rational theory what cannot be seen. For the similarity that exists between atoms and objects without any gaps is sufficient for these purposes. But these smallest of micro-objects could not form compounds even if they could move.

[60] Now, we must not propose that the infinite has a highest or a lowest point, an "up" or a "down." But we know that motion upward from where we stand into the space above our heads, which can be extended to infinity, can never appear to us identical with motion conceived of as downward from our point of reference, as being both upward and downward at once: this would be impossible to conceive of. So we can consider one infinite line of motion upward and one downward, even if we have watched countless times as an object that moves upward from our perspective passes our heads and reaches the feet of someone above us, or an object moving below our feet reaches the head of someone above us. For all relative motion can be thought of just the same as infinite in either direction.

[61] Moreover, atoms must all necessarily move with equal speed whenever they travel through empty space and encounter no resistance. The heavy ones should not be thought of as faster than the smaller and lighter ones, so long as nothing opposes them, nor should the small ones be considered faster than the large ones; each one possesses an equivalent motion so long as they find a passage large enough for them, irrespective of any upward or lateral motion which they acquire through collisions, or downward motion which comes from their own weight. To the extent that an atom persists on any path, it moves as fast as thought until something collides with it from outside or the weight of the atom itself overcomes the influence of some applied force.

[62] But when it comes to compounds, some will move faster than others, though the atoms within them move with equal speed. This is because atoms in a conglomerate move toward the same place in the shortest continuous interval of time, even if the mind cannot grasp the size of one such interval. But they are packed so close together that so far as the senses can perceive it, their collisions register as continuous motion. The additional assumption about what cannot be observed, that intervals of time marked out in theory will exhibit continuous motion, is not true when it comes to things like this. Everything that can be reasoned out in theory or perceived directly is true.

[63] Next we ought to survey what evidence is furnished by our senses and their impressions—since that is how we will obtain the most securely persuasive evidence—to the effect that the soul is a body composed of very fine parts, distributed throughout the whole mass of the body, most closely resembling a breath with a certain measure of thermal energy mixed in—resembling breath in one way, and heat in another. But there is one part of it that surpasses the others in the thinness of its particles, which is therefore more finely tuned in sync with the rest of the body. All the soul's abilities make this part manifest, as do its sensations, its healthy functioning, and everything whose loss amounts to death. It is also a necessary proposition that the soul possesses the greater part of all sense perception, [64] though it would not perceive if it weren't encased in the rest of the body in some way. And the rest of the body, furnishing the conditions of perception, in turn receives the cause of its sense perception furnished by this delicate part of the soul, having itself a certain sympathy with that part, though not obtaining the full extent of its powers. This is why when the soul departs,

the remaining body has no sensation. For it did not achieve the power of perception in itself, but was furnished with it through a congenital alignment with something else, which by way of its complementary power communicated sense experience directly to the rest of the body through motion—as soon as the soul's particles attained this sensitivity to perception, it distributed it through the rest of the body by virtue of its alignment and inter-connectedness with it, as I said.

[65] Consequently, when the soul is present in the body, it will never lose sensation, no matter what other parts might be lost. Even if some region of the soul should be lost when the flesh enveloping it should be destroyed in whole or in part, if the soul overall remains, so will sense perception. But when the last mass of atoms possessing the nature of the soul, however thinly stretched, finally departs, then the remaining body parts, both collectively and individually, will have no sense perception. And indeed, when the whole mass of the body is destroyed, the soul is scattered and no longer has the same abilities or moves in the same way, so that it achieves no sentience.

[66] It's impossible to maintain that the same sensory faculty inheres if the atoms are no longer in the same arrangement and no longer possess the same motion, when the parts that held it together and encased it, within which structure it had those movements, are no longer the same. [He says in his other writings that the soul is composed of the smoothest and roundest atoms, in both respects far surpassing fire. And there is a part of it that has no rational faculties, which is spread throughout the rest of the body—but the rational part is in the chest cavity, as is clear from fears and joys. Sleep occurs when the parts of the soul that are distributed throughout the whole bodily compound are either

stopped up or dispersed, and then collide with one another upon impact. And semen comes from every part of the body.]

[67] And it's necessary to consider in addition that when most ordinary people use the term "incorporeal," they are really thinking of things that exist in themselves. But what exists in itself can't be considered incorporeal except empty space. And empty space can neither act nor be acted upon: it simply provides a void for bodies to move through. So those who say that the soul is incorporeal are talking nonsense. If it were, it could neither act nor be acted upon, and we plainly see that both those capacities are attributes belonging to the soul.

[68] Next, if one refers all this reasoning about the soul to the touchstone of our impressions and sense perceptions, always bearing in mind the principles articulated in the beginning, he will see that what is contained in the general outline allows him to advance to specifics with sound and confident reasoning.

So now, shapes and colors and sizes and weights and all the other various things that are attributed to bodies incidentally (either to all things or only to visible things), and known by the senses themselves, cannot be thought of as existing by nature in themselves—for that is not possible to conceive. [69] Nor are they altogether nonexistent, nor are they some kind of separate entity that exists incorporeally apart from the object they are attached to, or as part of it. Instead the whole body derives its own permanent character from all such qualities, though they can't be heaped up in the way that actual masses combine to form a larger pile, made either from primary atoms or from any bodies that are themselves smaller than the larger whole—rather these bodies, as I say, only acquire their own permanent character out of the sum total of those attributes. And these qualities have their own properties and distinctions that follow on from the arrangement of the bodies they belong to, and are never separate from them, but rather are attributes grasped from the body by virtue of its being conceived as a whole.

[70] It also often happens that bodies acquire incidental and temporary attributes, which accompany them—these attributes are neither among those things which cannot be observed, nor are they incorporeal. As a result we apply to them the term "accidents" to make clear that they do not exhibit the behavior of the whole, which we call a "body" by taking account of the whole mass, nor that of the permanent features, without which it is not possible to conceive of a body at all. We give each accident its name with reference to certain effects that the whole thing has on us under particular conditions, [71] though they are never all seen to belong to the body at once, since the accidents are not permanent. And we must not exclude from our account of reality the manifest appearance that accidents do not have the character of the whole which they accompany, to which we truly give the name of "body," nor that of those permanent features that accompany the body. Nor should they be thought of as existing in themselves—for it is not even right to think that about the permanent attributes, let alone the accidents—instead, as is apparent, they ought to be thought of as coinciding with bodies, and neither accompanying them permanently nor again having the rank of things that exist in themselves or have their own nature: rather, whatever way our sense perception constructs their particular character, that is how they are seen to be.

[72] And this further point must be kept firmly in mind: we should not investigate time in the same way we do other things which belong to some underlying reality by deriving conclusions

from examining our own preconceptions: instead, we should consider the raw experience itself, according to which we call an interval of time either "short" or "long," making reference to our innate awareness. There's no need to prefer novel terms when we can make use of the ones that already exist in this domain, nor should we attribute some other thing to time, as if it had the same essential feature that we attach to the specific nature of time—for some people do that, too—but instead we ought to use language which connects time specifically to what is unique about it and measures it out in its own units. [73] There's no need of elaborate demonstrations or arguments to support this: we associate time with days and nights and the subdivisions of these, just as we do also to impressions and their absence, and motions and rest, thinking again about those aspects of them that we identify with the word "time." [He also says this in the second book of *On Nature* and in the *Larger Survey*.]

In addition to what has already been said, it's necessary to believe that the worlds, and all compounds shaped in the same kinds of form that we commonly observe, arose out of the infinite. They were all separated out with their distinctive compositions of atoms, be they larger or smaller, and they will all be dissolved again—some faster, some slower, under the influence of this or that force. [It is clear from this that he also considers worlds perishable when their parts change. Elsewhere he asserts that the earth is held up by the air.]

[74] Moreover we must believe by necessity that the worlds do not all have one kind of form. [He says himself in *On Nature* 12 that they vary in form: some are spherical, others are ovoid, and still others are of other shapes. But they do not have every kind of shape. Nor are they conscious organisms that have been

separated out from the totality of the infinite.] For no one could possibly prove that the seeds from which animals, and plants, and all the rest of the beings we observe are formed could be contained in one kind of world but not in another [nor could this be said of their means of rearing and nourishment. And the same reasoning applies to those things that exist on earth].

[75] Another necessary supposition is that human nature has learned a wide array and variety of things from the facts on the ground, which it has been compelled to accept. And reason later clarified and added to what nature discovered, though faster among some peoples and slower among others, while some made greater advances in certain time periods than in others. From this it may also be inferred that the names of things were not initially imposed by convention, but rather the natures of men themselves in their several ethnic groups experienced distinctive impressions and received their own perceptions of things, issuing bursts of air sent forth uniquely by each of those impressions and perceptions, which is how it ever came about that there are differences even from place to place within one ethnic group. [76] But next, within each group, shared clarifications emerged to make things less ambiguous and designate them more concisely through their common usage. When it came to matters that can't be observed, those who were aware of such things bestowed on their listeners mutually understood sounds, either driven from them spontaneously or arrived at by reason, offering the most generally intelligible explanation.

As for the trajectories of the celestial bodies overhead—their revolutions, their eclipses, their rising and setting, and everything that accompanies these—we should not imagine that they take place through the ministrations of any individual who organizes or appoints them while simultaneously possessing perfect bliss and immortality. [77] For effort and worry aren't in keeping with bliss; neither is anger nor special favor. They arise only in the context of weakness, fear, and mutual dependency. And anyway, we mustn't imagine that a spinning fireball adopts these movements according to some intention when it already possesses perfect joy: we should instead retain the full measure of dignity in the language we use to express our ideas in this area, so that no beliefs emerge to undermine that dignity. Otherwise, that contradiction alone will create in us the most severe psychological disquiet. For which reason it's imperative we maintain the belief that these bodies are executing necessary movements and rotations in which they were implicated from the very beginning of the world's origin, and which they have retained since then.

[78] What's more, we must consider it the business of natural philosophy to specify precise explanations of the most serious matters, upon which our own happiness depends, as well as on contemplating the true nature of these celestial bodies, and whatever facilitates clarity on that subject.

And furthermore, we should not accept multiple explanations or alternative theories in this domain: it is not in the nature of bliss or immortality to admit of anything resembling unrest or dispute, and we are perfectly capable of grasping this simple truth.

[79] But when it comes to individual areas of research, as regards settings and risings and revolutions and eclipses and whatever belongs to that family of subjects, further knowledge does not conduce to any greater well-being: experts in these narrow fields, if they are ignorant of the nature of things or of the most important explanations, are afflicted with just the same anxieties as if they knew nothing about these matters at all—and more

often than not with others besides, since they are astonished that from their store of knowledge they can arrive at no resolution or management of the most important things.

So if we discover more than one feasible explanation for revolutions, settings, risings, eclipses, and all such tendencies, as we did in other subsidiary areas, [80] we shouldn't think that for want of information in those areas we will fall short of accuracy, insofar as it conduces to our serenity and wellness. When we work out explanations concerning the celestial bodies or anything else that's not immediately apparent from our sense impressions, we should consider how many ways there are for similar phenomena to present themselves to us, disdaining those who can't distinguish between what happens consistently according to a single logic and what can happen for various reasons, because they overlook the fact that our sense data comes to us from a distance and have no understanding of the conditions for serenity. So then, if we can accept that the same thing might happen in multiple ways, then when we discern it happening in various manners we will be just as serene as if we knew that it happens in this or that way.

[81] In addition to all these considerations, it must be kept in mind that the most overpowering unease possible in the human psyche arises from considering these celestial bodies blessed or immortal while at the same time attributing to them contradictory desires, actions, and motivations, and moreover holding some terrible expectation about eternity or suspecting it on the basis of myths, or even fearing the oblivion that will come over us in death (as if it will exist for us), and suffering from these misapprehensions not because of some rigorously considered belief so much as some irrational tic of their subconscious. So if they can't restrain these fears, they will suffer the same or even worse unease than

afflicts people who give such matters only the occasional passing thought. [82] Serenity consists in dispelling all such fears and bearing the most important elements of the bigger picture continually in mind.

From which it follows that one ought to attend to one's immediate impressions, whether universal or particular, making use of the most vivid and immediate sensations according to each of the standards of truth. If we hold fast to these ideas, we will arrive at the means of dispelling and explaining away every psychological disturbance or fear, heading off the most extreme fears that grip everyone else with explanations about the celestial bodies and all the rest.

These are the top-line items that I've sketched out for you concerning the entirety of nature, Herodotus. [83] By consequence, if this account is firmly and clearly assimilated so that it becomes effective knowledge, I think that even someone who does not proceed to full study of all the details will acquire a mental vigor incomparably greater than that of other men. He will be able to produce a clean account of many details I hammered out in my complete treatment of the subject. Memorizing this summary and referring to it constantly will help.

They are so composed that even a student already well advanced in satisfactory or even extensive clarification of the minor points, if he refers back to these general principles, will obtain a comprehensive overall view of more or less the entirety of nature, whereas those who have not altogether completed an exhaustive study of nature will be able to silently revise, at the speed of thought, the most important overall points for soothing their troubled minds.

The Letter to Pythocles
(Diogenes Laertius 10.83–116)

Here Epicurus gives a bravura display of possible explanations for various celestial and meteorological phenomena, inventing hypothesis after hypothesis about how atomic interactions might explain weather patterns and astronomical observations. His idea of "multiple explanations," hinted at in the previous letter, involves resting content with any and all explanations that are not incompatible with the observable phenomena (if they are incompatible, it's called a "refutation," antimarturēsis).

Viable explanations only need to be consistent with what can be observed, even if those explanations are not consistent with each other. So, for example, solar eclipses might be caused when the sun is obscured by another body passing in between us and it ("occultation"), or else they might be caused by the sun's fire temporarily going out altogether ("extinction"). Possibly Epicurus thinks that these speculations are all equally true, even if mutually exclusive, or that it's meaningless to speak of "truth" and "falsehood" where no definite knowledge is possible. More likely, though, he thinks that only one explanation is correct in any given instance, but we can't always be sure which one. Sometimes he argues that the same phenomenon can be produced in different ways at different times.

The main point is not to go beyond what is warranted by the data: from our present standpoint, at least, we only have so much information to go on, and we shouldn't feign certainty where none is justified. It's enough to put the mind at ease if we can rule out the more fantastical ideas that the general public fret over, especially when they take portents in the sky as harbingers or evidence of some god intervening in human affairs. Beyond that, we will attain serenity if we refrain from endorsing any one physical theory when others can't be conclusively ruled out.

Epicurus to Pythocles

Greetings,

[84] Cleon brought me a letter from you in which you continued to express your goodwill toward me, in a manner befitting my own sincere care for you. You were making a plausible effort at committing to memory those arguments that lead most concisely to a life of bliss, to which end you implored me to send you a neatly written summary of my reasoning concerning the heavenly bodies, so that you could memorize it more easily—since, as you say, it is dispersed throughout my other written works in a manner that makes it hard to remember, though you refer to them constantly. I received this request of yours with pleasure; it fills me with equally pleasurable hopes for your future. [85] Having

written everything else required of me, I will produce the summary you asked for, which will be useful for many others as well, especially those who have only just had their first taste of genuine natural science and those who are wrapped up in some project more demanding than what is entailed in a standard education. Make good use of it, and once you have it memorized, go back over it regularly in detail along with the rest of the things I sent to Herodotus in that brief overview.

First of all, remember that just like all other studies, knowledge about celestial bodies has no other purpose—whether we make reference to it in connection with other discussions or consider it in its own right—than peace of mind and secure belief. [86] We cannot bring about the impossible by force, and we should not stick to the same kind of exhaustive study as the other sciences, such as those concerning living things or the resolution of other problems in natural science—such as the principle that all things are composed of bodies and that which is fundamentally intangible, or that the foundational elements of things are indivisible, and all such proposals, which admit of only one explanation that agrees with the phenomena we experience. In this field, there is a range of accounts about the origin and essence of the celestial bodies that conform with the evidence of our senses.

[87] For we must not proceed in our study of nature from arbitrary premises and axioms that we ourselves lay down, but rather follow where the observed phenomena lead us. The last thing we need in our lives is baseless and empty ideas: what we need is to live without unnecessary fracas. So everything will proceed smoothly as soon as the whole thing has been sorted out according to a range of explanations, each one of which conforms to what has been observed, so that one can put each matter to

rest appropriately once it has been properly and convincingly explained. But if one picks and chooses among explanations, though each conforms to the observable phenomena, then clearly he has fallen short of comprehensive study and lapsed into myth. Some of the things we observe down here in our domain furnish indications of what is unfolding in the heavens. We can explain how these indications come about, but not the phenomena we actually observe among the heavenly bodies, which may arise in a range of ways. [88] But we should closely analyze each event that presents itself to us and distinguish it from the other events that accompany it, whose origin in a variety of causes is not contradicted by the experience we have in our own sphere.

A world is a bounded region of space, containing stars, an earth, and all the phenomena comprised therein. It is cut off and distinct from the limitless exterior and it is contained within either a thin or dense boundary. It is either revolving or stationary, contained within a circle or triangle or whatever other perimeter—each of these may be accepted, as none of the phenomena in this world, where no boundary can be observed, contradicts any shape the boundary might take.

[89] It is also possible to grasp that such worlds are limitless in number, and that such a world can come into being both within another world and in the worldscape, which is the name we give to the space between worlds: a largely empty space, though not, as some maintain, an enormous and totally empty void, since certain raw materials do flow from one world or area of the worldscape, or several, causing in the process various conjunctions, transfers, slipstreams, and rearrangements from place to place, little by little, as chance would have it. And a persistent stream of the appropriate particles to the right destination, once

they attain sufficient stability and development and settle into foundations that can host them, leads to the creation of a new world. [90] For what is required for a world to emerge is not simply a heap or a vortex from whose cavity it will grow (by necessity, as some think), until it makes contact with another world. Though this is what one so-called natural philosopher claims, it conflicts with the observed phenomena. A sun and a moon and all the rest of the stars did not first form independently, then get absorbed by our world and all the parts that hold it together; they were all formed and grew in conjunction [along with the earth and the sea] by the gradual accretion of certain spiraling microparticles, whether gaseous or fiery in nature, or both. *This* is what the evidence of our senses indicates.

[91] The size of the sun and the rest of the stars is as large as it seems relative to us. [He also says this in *On Nature* Book 11, arguing that if the size were reduced by the distance, then the brightness would be reduced still more.] For there is no other distance more proportional to this size. In itself, however, it may be larger than it looks to us, or slightly smaller, or exactly the same size. We can observe the same effect in fires on earth when we observe them from a distance. Every objection to this portion of the science can be easily overcome, as I have shown in *On Nature*.

[92] It is possible that the rising and setting of the sun and moon and the rest of the stars occurs when they are successively ignited and extinguished, if the nature of their surroundings in the relevant locations, east and west, is such as to bring that about: none of the observed phenomena contradicts it. But it may also be a consequence of their visible position above the earth or the passage of another body in front of them: nothing we can observe contradicts that, either. It is not impossible that their

motion is caused by the rotation of the whole sky, but it may also be that the sky stands still while they themselves move along an orbit imposed on them by necessity since they first rose when the world originally came into being. [93][1]

It is possible that the retrograde motions of the sun and the moon are caused by the slant of the sky itself, which is imposed from time to time. Or they may equally be the result of air resistance, or a shortage of the material necessary to propel them, which is burned off. Alternatively, rotational motion may have been imparted to these stars at the origin of the world, so that they travel in a kind of spiral. Not one manifest fact clashes with any such explanation, or any other in the same family, if one sticks to what is possible and proceeds from the relevant details to each explanation that harmonizes with the observed phenomena—and if one refuses to be intimidated by the groveling contrivances of the astrologers.

[94] And the alternate waxing and waning of the moon could be a result of its own motion; it could equally come from the configuration of the surrounding air, or yet again from its position behind other bodies, or any number of other means which the phenomena furnished by the moon's appearance down here might suggest to us—so long as one doesn't become enamored of one unitary explanation and pronounce the others worthless, failing to realize what kind of understanding is possible for humans to attain and what kinds are impossible, leading to an aspiration to understand the incomprehensible. Likewise, the

---

1   At this point there is a brief section of text has been mangled and rendered incomplete in transmission: it goes something like "With the most extreme heat through a certain distribution of fire, which always travels to adjacent regions."

moon could shine with its own light, or derive it from the sun. [95] Here on earth we see that many bodies have their own light, and many derive it from others—and none of the phenomena we observe in the heavens prevents either of these from being the case, if we always bear in mind the various alternative possibilities and hold all the hypotheses and explanations that follow on from the phenomena in our minds at once, rather than digging up others that aren't relevant for no reason other than to tilt the scales in favor of one or the other unitary explanation. The appearance of a face in the moon could be a result of rearrangement in its parts, or the placement of other bodies in front of it, or whatever other means could be reasonably inferred from what we observe. [96] When it comes to celestial phenomena, anyone who abandons pursuit of these kinds of explanations, in stubborn rebellion against the manifest evidence, will never be able to attain true inner peace.

Eclipses of the sun and of the moon could happen when they are extinguished, as we sometimes observe happening here on earth; and we already know they could be a result of some other body passing in front of them, whether the earth or one of the unobservable ones. In this way we always want to take into account all explanations that are consistent with each other and join together all of them that aren't impossible. [In *On Nature* Book 12 he adds to this that the sun is eclipsed when the moon leaves it in shadow, and the moon is eclipsed by the earth's shadow—or else eclipse may be the result of increased distance. [97] Diogenes the Epicurean says the same in his *Selected Writings*.]

And it must still be accepted that there is an order to the heavenly cycles, of the kind we see inhering also in what happens all around us. And nothing divine should ever be brought into the discussion: the divine should be kept undisturbed and altogether blissful. If this rule is not followed, every rationale concerning the heavenly bodies will fall into useless incoherence, as has already happened to some people who can't lay hold of a workable method, so that they lapse into inanities in their belief that many distinct things are the result of one cause, rejecting what should be accepted and getting carried away into inconceivable fantasies, while refusing to make an overall survey of phenomena which they should be able to take as indicators of truth.

[98] The variable length of days and nights may result from the alternating speed and slowness of the sun's movements relative to the earth as a consequence of the variable terrain it has to pass through, some of which it traverses faster and some more slowly—a phenomenon we also observe in certain terrestrial situations. Whatever we say about the heavenly bodies should also be in harmony with these principles. Those who apply only one of these explanations are fighting in vain against the evidence and have failed to consider how it is possible for humanity to arrive at such knowledge.

Meteorological indicators might be the result of simple coincidence, as we sometimes see happening among animals on earth, or of alternations and exchanges of pressure in the air. Neither of these explanations conflicts with the phenomena. [99] But which one of these several causes really brings about each instance is not possible to discover.

Clouds might be formed through the compression of air under the influence of wind, or through the entanglement of the right kind of atoms that adhere to one another and produce the necessary effect, or through the collocation of the necessary streams of earth and water, or by many various other means of composition that would not be inadequate for cloud formation. Water might be produced from them when they rub together, or when they are transformed. [100] Rain might occur when clouds are swelled by an influx of air, the more forceful of them coming from those masses that are built up enough to produce them. Thunder might come from winds that are shut up in the hollow centers of the clouds, as we see in our cisterns, or from explosions of the fire within them when tossed by winds, or it also might occur when clouds are broken apart and dissolved, or when shards of frozen clouds break off and collide. This field, like the whole subject, is conducive to a range of multiple explanations, all of them indicated by the phenomena. [101] Lightning, too, can come about in many ways: through friction and collision between clouds, when a tear in one of them lets slip the kind of combustible body that can produce a lightning bolt, or when the clouds are prompted by winds to emit those particles that give forth the appropriate glow, or when those particles are forced out by the friction produced in clouds either by one another or by the winds. Or else perhaps the glow of light scattered from the stars is trapped in the clouds, then driven out by their motion and by the winds so that it passes between them. Or else the most finely strained particles of light may be filtered out through the clouds and moved through them, in which case the cloud is set on fire and produces thunderclaps as well, or else the tension of movement and extreme pressure forces the wind to combust. [102] Then again it may be fissures in the clouds made by the wind that allow those atoms that produce fire to escape and give off the appearance of a lightning bolt. And we could easily survey many other ways it could happen, as long as we stick to the phenomena and can come up with something that conforms to them. Now in these kinds of cloud configurations, lightning strikes before thunder, because the kind of material that produces the lightning is forced out right as the wind hits, and later on the wind, trapped inside the cloud, gives off the rumble of thunder. But if they both occur at once, it is because the lightning travels toward us with greater speed and the thunder follows after, [103] just as when we watch certain people striking each other from a distance. Thunderbolts can occur when multiple wind currents meet, leading to severe compression and conflagration, or when one part of a cloud is broken off and sent falling violently into the lower regions, the fracture having occurred through the tighter pressure in the adjacent regions produced by the tightly packed clouds. It can also occur as a direct result of the fire trapped in the clouds being expelled—which is also a way for thunder to occur—as the fire is fed increasingly by the air and becomes more abundant, breaking out of the cloud since the constant pressure makes it impossible for it to go back to the adjacent regions (this is most often the case near mountain peaks, where thunderbolts most frequently fall). [104] And thunderbolts can be produced in many other ways—only let myth be dispensed with. And it *will* be dispensed with, if one sticks to the observed phenomena to draw inferences about what is not observed.

Whirlwinds can happen through the descent of clouds into the lower region, forced into a column and carried on downward on a heavy current of abundant wind, as the cloud is simultaneously forced sideways by an external wind. They can also be produced when the wind curves around into a circular pattern and a quantity of air pushes downward from above. Alternatively a large gust of many winds may occur and find no lateral outlet because of the density of the surrounding air. [105] And once the whirlwind is forced down onto the ground it starts to produce cyclones, as dictated by the manner in which the winds produced it. And when it hits the water, it produces eddies.

Earthquakes can occur when wind is shut up under the ground, and when it is distributed among small masses of earth and moves among them, at which point it produces a vibration in the earth. This wind is either trapped from outside, or from the collapse of foundations in the cavernous regions beneath the earth, which compels the trapped air to produce a wind. And the transfer of motion that occurs among the fallen rocks of several foundations, if they encounter sufficient resistance from a critical mass of compacted earth, can in itself create an earthquake. [106] And these kinds of motion can come about in many other ways.

Winds are sometimes formed through the gradual accumulation of foreign matter seeping into the air bit by bit, and through an abundant admixture of water. The rest of the winds are formed when some of them fall into the earth's many cavities and get split up within them.

Hail is produced through powerful condensation, when gaseous particles from all sides collect into drops, and through a more moderate condensation of certain fluids, causing them to come together and break apart at the same time, so that their simultaneous condensation and rupture freezes both the parts and the whole. [107] It is not impossible that the spherical shape of hailstones is a result of their extremities having been melted down on all sides and their constant contact with either gaseous or fluid particles on all sides.

Snow can be produced when a thin stream of water is poured out of the clouds through passageways of appropriate proportions, under the constant influence of extreme winds on the right kind of cloud, whereupon this rain freezes on its downward course because of the sharp drop in temperature in the regions below the clouds. Or if evenly and thinly dispersed clouds become frozen, snow might be expelled when clouds that are saturated with fluid get packed alongside each other. Such clouds produce hail when forced together, which happens most often in the springtime. [108] And friction between frozen clouds can also produce a quantity of snow, which may be produced in other ways as well.

Dew is produced when the particles that can produce such moisture gather together from the air. It may also be created when such particles are carried upward either from damp regions or from those saturated with water (where dew is most likely to occur) and then come back together, combining their moisture and returning back to the lower areas, as we also observe many similar processes in our daily experience. [109] And frost is produced in much the same way as dew, when certain particles freeze in the presence of cold air.

Ice is produced when the round atoms in water are ejected while the pointed and uneven ones are packed together, or by the accretion of those types from outside which, when driven together, freeze the water once they have displaced enough of the round types.

Rainbows are produced by the projection of the sun's rays through hydrated air, or else through a particular affinity between light and air, which creates the distinctive conditions for producing the relevant colors, all at once or one by one. And when this light in turn is refracted through the neighboring air, it takes on these same colors—as we observe when its parts are illuminated.

[110] And the reason for its curved appearance is that its distance from our standpoint of observation is the same in every direction—or else the atoms in the air have taken on a certain density, or those in the clouds, derived from the same air, are arranged together in such a manner as to appear in this curved shape.

A halo floats around the moon because air is arrayed around it all the way to its borders; alternatively, the air lifts up the currents from the moon equally in all directions up to the point where it deposits a cloudy ring that never completely breaks free. Or else it lifts up the air around the moon in equal measure on all sides into a thick circle around it. [111] This happens in particular areas either because of a current that forces itself in from outside or a quantity of heat that finds sufficient channels to travel in and accomplish it.

Comets are a consequence either of fire gathering together among the celestial bodies at certain intervals under the right conditions, or of movement over time in the heavens themselves above us, so that such stars appear, or else at various times the bodies themselves are forced into our field of vision and become observable. And they disappear whenever the opposite eventualities cause them to. [112] It happens that certain stars revolve in place, not only—as some say—because that part of the world is fixed in place while the rest revolves around it, but also because a vortex of air surrounds it and keeps it from spinning like the rest, or else because there is no suitable fuel in the surrounding regions as there is in the place where they are observed. It could also arise from plenty of other causes, if someone managed to work one out that conformed to the observable phenomena. The reason why some stars wander relative to the others which hold their positions (if indeed that is how they move) [113] might be because they have to by necessity since they were set in a circular motion at the origin of the universe, so that some are carried along by the same rotational force along parallel tracks, whereas others are carried on different, anomalous tracks. It is also possible that the quality of air fluctuates from region to region, so that those with regular air quality carry them along in uniform motion as they burn continuously, whereas in regions with irregular density they exhibit the anomalous motion we observe. But those who put forward a single explanation, when the phenomena invite a variety of accounts, are acting deranged. They have allowed themselves to be led to inappropriate conclusions by those who put forward pointless astrological reasoning about illusory causes, pressing the divine into service and so rendering it incoherent. [114] It has sometimes happened that a particular star is observed to fall behind the others, because it is traveling more slowly than the others in its proper orbit, or because it has been pressed backward in the opposite direction by the same driving vortex. It may also be that some stars cover a greater distance, and others cover less, in the course of the same revolution. To attribute these sorts of things to one simple cause is a mark of the sort of person that wants to overawe the general public with signs and portents.

Those stars which are said to "fall" may do so either because of mutual friction between the stars themselves or because some parts become detached under the influence of wind, as we also suggested in regards to lightning bolts. [115] It may also be the result of collision among the atoms that produce fire, when material in that family of atoms is produced and brings this about, so that the motion imparted by this initial impulse dictates the ensuing trajectories. It may also be that an accumulation of wind in certain foggy masses gets trapped and explodes, which then punctures the surrounding material and carries it to whatever location is dictated by the application of that initial force. There are many other ways of bringing this about that do not involve mythological activity.

The behavior of certain animals occasionally coincides with the indicators of weather patterns by an accidental correlation of timing: for the animals cannot impose any constraints on the weather to become stormy, nor is there any divine overseer who observes the patterns of these animals' movement and then executes their meteorological directives. [116] Not even a moderately fortunate life-form would be afflicted by such inanities, let alone one possessed of perfect happiness.

So then, Pythocles: keep all these things in mind. They will keep you well protected from mythology and enable you to understand all related matters. Give yourself over in particular to the study of causes and of the infinite and that whole class of things, then to human experiences and the sources of truth, and why we have reason to consider such things. A comprehensive study of these things will be the easiest way to explain more minor details. But those who are not passionately interested in such things have not understood them or reached the goal that should have been the purpose of studying to begin with.

The Letter to Menoeceus
(Diogenes Laertius 10.121–35)

If there is a piece of writing that has defined how Epicurus is remembered, it is probably this short letter. Here is where he lays out the consequences of atomic theory and materialism for daily life, proposing that the soul evaporates when the body expires and so "death is nothing to us." It follows that the highest thing we can achieve is happiness in this life, although Epicurus thinks this still means behaving with all the typical virtues that a Roman or Greek reader would have already endorsed—courage, moderation, prudence, and so forth. What's more, Epicurus argues, the goodness of those virtues can be explained by the very fact that they help us make life as enjoyable and peaceable as possible.

Epicurus to Menoeceus

Greetings,

[122] No young man should ever put off doing philosophy, nor should anyone who's already in the habit age out of it as the years go by. No one is too mature or immature to look after the health of his mind. To say it's not yet time for philosophy, or that the time has passed, is like saying it's too early or too late to live a good life. That's why it's essential for everyone, young and old, to do philosophy: so that a man may stay fresh in matters of quality as he ages, adorned with the grace of what's come before, and so that a young man may be wise beyond his years on account of his fearlessness at what is to come. So we must take care to cultivate the good life. If we are already living it, we have everything. If it still eludes us, we do everything we can to attain it.

[123] Take care that you persist in those practices that I constantly used to urge on you: consider them the building blocks of living well. First of all, believe that every god is living, incorruptible, and blessedly happy (this is the universally acceptable account of what deity means) and never attribute any quality to them that is foreign to incorruptibility or incommensurate with their happiness: you should believe whatever enables them to retain the bliss that comes with being incorruptible. Gods exist, and our knowledge of that fact is manifestly clear, but they are nothing like what most people think of them, since most people don't even maintain consistent ideas about them. Impiety amounts not to denying what the general public believes about the gods, but to believing it. [124] These assertions that people make about the gods are not innate convictions but inaccurate

assumptions, which teach them that the gods do harm to bad men and reward good men. This is because of their bias in favor of their own virtues; they readily embrace what is like them and are baffled by anything foreign.

Get used to believing that death is nothing to us. Every good and every evil consists in sentience—but death is the loss of sentience. As a result, a correct understanding that death is nothing to us renders our own mortality enjoyable, not by infinitely extending our time here but by dispelling our desire for immortality. [125] For there's nothing fearsome in life once you've truly grasped that nothing is fearsome about *not* living. So only a fool would say that he's afraid of death not because it will hurt him once it arrives, but because the expectation of it hurts him now as it approaches. There's no point in fretting over the prospect of something that can't bother you once it comes. So death, the most chilling fear that afflicts us, is actually nothing to us, since when we are present death is not, and when death is present we are not. So it's of no consequence to those who are living or to those who have died, since for the former it doesn't exist, and the latter no longer exist themselves.

But the general public sometimes avoids death as if it were the supreme misfortune, while at other times they opt for it as a reprieve from the other misfortunes of life.[1] [126] Whereas the wise man is neither unwilling to live nor afraid of not living; he neither resents being alive nor considers it a misfortune not to be. Similarly he will not aim for the largest helping of food but the most enjoyable: in the same way he savors not the longest

---

1 The Greek text is missing some words here; the sense, reconstructed in the translation, is clear enough.

time possible but the sweetest. And anyone who urges a young man to live admirably, and an old man to take his leave gracefully, is being silly—not only because life is desirable in itself, but because living and dying well are as one. Worse by far to be the sort of person that claims it's better not to have been born and, "once born, to make haste and rush to the gates of Hades."[2]

[127] If anyone makes such claims in earnest, why doesn't he take his leave of life? That course of action is readily available to him, if he is firmly resolved to take it. But if it's all just a routine, it's a pointless one, and quite inappropriate for the subject matter.

Let it be kept in mind that the future is neither entirely within, nor entirely outside of, our control. This way we will neither await it with total certainty, nor despair of it ever coming altogether.

It should further be reckoned that, among our desires, some are natural and some are fruitless. Of the natural ones, some are necessary and others merely natural. And of the necessary ones, some are necessary for our well-being, others for the comfort of our bodies, still others simply to sustain its life. [128] Unwavering contemplation of these things can inform every choice and aversion, directing them all toward the health of the body and the serenity of the mind, since this is the final goal of a blessed life. That's why we do everything: so that we will be neither afflicted nor troubled. And the moment this condition emerges in us, it parts the storm clouds of the soul, since there is nothing else left for our organism to go hunting after that would further complete the satisfaction of body or mind. For we only stand in need of

---

2   This is a quote from the sixth-century BC elegiac poet Theognis (425, 427).

pleasure when we are afflicted by the lack of it: when we are not so afflicted, we feel no need for pleasure. And for this reason we assert that pleasure is the source and purpose of a blessed life. [129] It is the first good thing we know from birth, from which arises our every preference and aversion, and we return to it when we use experience as the standard against which we measure every value. And because it is the first good thing we know from birth, it is also the standard according to which we do not pursue every pleasure. To the contrary, there are times when we forgo many pleasures, since otherwise even greater discomfort will result from them. We also consider many afflictions preferable to pleasures, in all cases where a more intense pleasure will follow them after we have endured them for a long time. Every pleasure, then, is inherently good by reason of its natural attractiveness to us, but not all of them are advisable to pursue. And though every affliction is also bad, not all of them should be avoided. [130] What is appropriate is to evaluate all these things by weighing and considering pluses and minuses. For sometimes we treat a good thing as if it were evil, and vice versa. And we consider self-sufficiency a major boon, not exactly so we can always get by with just a few things, but so that *if* we don't have many things, we will be satisfied with just a few—since we are genuinely convinced that those who need abundance least are the ones who can enjoy it most, and that natural things are easiest to procure, while inane ones are hardest. After all, simple food gives just as much pleasure as an extravagant meal the moment that the pain of deprivation has been alleviated, [131] and even plain barley cakes with water can furnish the most exquisite pleasure when we acquire them in an hour of real need. So getting used to simple meals, no more extravagant than is essential for healthy nutrition and the necessary amenities of life, makes a man hardy and stands us in better stead when we do enjoy the occasional luxury, steeling us against the fear of chance.

So then, when we say that pleasure is the end goal, we don't mean those pleasures enjoyed in reckless abandon by those consumed with material delights, as imagined by certain ignorant people or those who dispute or misunderstand our position. We mean freedom from bodily affliction and mental disquiet. [132] It's not constant drinking and partying, and not the fleshly enjoyment of women or boys, nor the taste of fish and other delicacies offered by an overloaded table, that creates a pleasurable life. It's sober reasoning and inspection of the cause for every choice or aversion, which dispels all the fanciful ideas that lead to the majority of all psychological disturbances. And the source of all this, the greatest good thing of all, is discernment. Which is why discernment ranks even higher than philosophy, since it generates the rest of the virtues and teaches that living enjoyably is impossible without living prudently, nobly, and righteously—nor is living prudently, nobly, and righteously possible without living enjoyably. The virtues and the life of pleasure are twins from birth, and pleasurable living is inseparable from the virtues.

[133] Who do you think could be superior to a man that believes holy things about the gods and remains unafraid of death in all circumstances? He has factored in the end goal of nature, seeing that the maximum limit of those good things necessary and conducive to well-being is within reach, and that misfortune is either fleeting in duration or moderate in severity, and laughing at the idea, quite common among some people, that fate is the master of everything. He believes instead that some things are a consequence of chance, and others are up to us. He can see that

necessity is impossible to avert, and luck is constantly changing, whereas we are sovereign over whatever is up to us, and that is the only domain in which moral censure or its opposite can apply. [134] It would be better to believe the stories they tell about gods than to submit to the determinism of fate proposed by natural philosophers. The former holds out hope of divine mercy by way of honors and supplication; the latter posits that fate is impossible to supplicate. Nor does he think fate is a god, as the general public does—since nothing disordered can be done by the hand of a god—nor that fate is an uncertain cause. He does not think fate provides anything, either good or bad, that will furnish mankind with a happy life, though it may orchestrate major advantages and disadvantages in our initial circumstances. [135] The right-thinking man believes that bad luck with understanding is better than good luck without it, since it is better if what is judged noble in our actions is not worked out by chance.

So then, see that you studiously practice these and all related attitudes day and night, alone and with a like-minded companion, and you will never be alarmed by visions or dreams. You will live instead like a god among men. For a man who lives with immortal prizes is like no living mortal.

PART II

Selections from Lucretius,
De Rerum Natura

Book I.265–328

Lucretius addresses the potential objection that atoms cannot be seen, meaning it is impossible to verify their existence directly through sense perception.

So then. Though I've made it clear that nothing
Can be called forth out of nothing, and
That likewise nothing made can be recalled
To nonexistence—still, perhaps this doubt
Will start to give you pause at what I say:
The rudiments of things cannot be seen.
But keep in mind the many other objects
[270] Which we must admit as being real
Despite the fact that they're invisible.
First, wind, which when whipped up exerts a force
That can collide and meet with other bodies,
Sending huge ships slipping through the waves

49

And carrying the clouds along their paths,
Or sprinting over fields in a tornado,
Scattering massive trees across the plains,
Pounding the hills with forest-breaking blasts.
[275] So on it rages with its bitter shrieks
And eerie moans across the dark sea's face.
So hidden particles must be at work—
Invisible, but not miraculous.
Over the sea and earth, among the clouds,
They sweep and eddy, whipping without warning
[280] Into a whirlwind, wreaking further havoc.
So water, too, is carried gently on
In streams, when suddenly a river surges,
Swollen to bursting by a heavy rain
That gushes from the distant mountain peaks
To toss aside the woods and groves in splinters.
[285] Not even sturdy bridges can withstand
The sudden strength of rushing water: so
The river rushes in, bulked up by rain,
With the full power of the roaring flood,
Dispensing mayhem everywhere it goes,
Rolling huge boulders underneath its streams,
Tossing aside whatever blocks its path.
[290] The winds and breezes must be buoyed onward
Just like rivers; they come rolling down
As rivers do, gathering strength en route,
Pushing things forward as they barrel on
In gusty blasts, or snatching up debris
To wrap them in a whirlwind's breakneck torque.
It follows that the winds are also made

[295] Of hidden particles, for their effects
And tendencies are found to rival those
Of rivers, which are plainly made of matter.
Then moreover, we can also smell
A wide array of odors; all the same,
At no point do we find that we can watch them
Entering our noses. We cannot see heat
[300] Or use our eyes to spot the chill of cold,
Nor do we tend to watch the path of voices—
All of which must by nature, just the same,
Be objects made of matter, since they can
Make contact with our senses. Making contact,
Touching or being touched: these are the things
Nothing except an object can achieve.
[305] Then you have clothes, which, when you hang them up
Along the shoreline where the breakers crash,
Grow damp. But if you stretch the same clothes out
Beneath the sun, then they dry out. The moisture
Soaks them unseen, and wicks away unseen
When heat approaches. So, it follows that
The moisture is diffused in tiny drops
[310] That no eye could conceivably observe.
Moreover, as the sun repeats its circuit
Year on year, the ring around your finger
Wanes away within; the steady drip
Of water hollows out a cave; a plough,
Though forged of curving iron, wears away
In secret as the soil grinds it down.
[315] And pavements can be smoothed beneath the feet
Of crowds, as we observe. Plus, there are statues

By the city gates, whose hands of bronze,
Which passersby have clasped to show respect,
Display the marks of daily wear and tear.
We notice all these signs of diminution
Once the bulk is visibly ground down.
[320] But in the moment, when the metal breaks
And falls away, the weakness of our sight
Prevents us by our nature from observing.
Finally, the things that nature builds
By gradual accretion, day by day
And bit by bit—no eye is sharp enough
That it can see the way she makes them grow.
Nor is there any gaze intent enough
[325] To watch the work of age, or of decay.
When cliffs jut out on high above the waves
And hang there in precarious suspension,
Eaten at slowly by corroding brine,
How much of them is lost, and when it's lost,
You cannot tell. The works that nature does,
She does with matter that cannot be seen.

Book II.216–293

This controversial passage puts forward the idea of a "swerve," a random deviation in atomic movement that makes free will and conscious choice possible (setting Lucretius's Epicureanism apart on this point from the fatalism of the Stoics, and the determinism of Democritus). Scholars debate whether this idea really originated with Epicurus, and whether the swerve is supposed to happen any time anyone makes an intentional choice, or if it only happened once to set the chain of reactions going that would eventually produce the various worlds.

We must be sure you grasp another point:
When particles are shooting down through space,
Although their weight propels them in straight lines,
At random times and places, suddenly,
They deviate just slightly from their paths
[220] By just so much as you could call a twitch—

Since otherwise, if they were not inclined
To waver off their paths, then everything
Would tumble down forever through the void
Like raindrops in a downpour, never meeting,
Never making contact or colliding.
Nature's raw materials would fall
Through endless wastes, and nothing would be made.
[225] You might think certain heavy particles,
By falling faster than the lighter ones,
Would hit them from above, and fill the void
By generating chain reactions. No:
This line of thought will lead you far astray.
[230] When objects fall through water or through air,
The speed with which they fall depends on weight,
Because the water's fluid substance, and
The delicate consistency of air
Can only slow each object down so much:
They yield more readily to heavy things.
[235] But space is utterly without resistance.
Nowhere is there force on any side
To slow the fall: the void will always yield.
It must, by nature, on account of which
Unequal weights must fall with equal speed
[240] Through empty space. No sudden contact, then,
Or automatic meeting from above
Can ever break the uniformity
Of motion, letting nature get to work.
And so, the paths of atoms have to bend,
If only slightly, just enough. Too much
Would make atomic motion angular,

[245] Which our observed experience refutes.
For plain and ready evidence can show
That weights will never fall in slanted lines
If dropped from elevated vantage points
And left to plummet of their own accord.
They never waver so far off their paths
That we can watch and see them deviate.
But who could ever possibly perceive,
With total certainty, that no slight curve
[250] Disturbs their downward motion? After all,
If every motion follows from the last,
And every movement that occurs is linked
To every other by necessity,
If nothing ever deviates or jogs
From its original trajectory,
Or breaks the bonds of fate, which lock the world
Within a chain of causes and effects
[255] Eternally, then how could souls be free?
And yet they are, in every place on earth
Where living beings breathe. Again I say:
Free will defies the fates. How could it be
That each man goes wherever free will leads,
Not at some predetermined time or place,
His changing course mapped out by destiny,
[260] But as his independent mind decrees?
No one could doubt that each man's own free will
Provides his source of motion, branching out
From deep within to animate the limbs.
And can't you see as well that when the gates
Spring open at the racetrack, even horses

Cannot instantly break out and run,
[265] Despite their sharp desire and their strength?
The impulse has to spur their bulky frames
And make its way to all extremities
Before the body can obey the mind.
And so, you see the resolution formed
First in the heart, and in the willing soul,
[270] From which it then proceeds to animate
The body and the limbs. It's quite unlike
The movement we experience when shoved
By someone else, whenever outward pressure
Forces us to move. When that occurs,
[275] The body lurches on unwillingly
Until our will can get a hold of it.
So, do you see that though external force
And jostling crowds can carry us along,
And often sweep us up, within our chests
There is a kind of strength that steadies us
[280] And gives us power to resist? Its will
Can ripple through the body's every limb
And pull us out of freefall into rest.
And so, the elementary particles,
You must admit, conceal within themselves
[285] An inward source of motion all their own.
Our own free movement is derived from theirs,
Since nothing comes from nothing, as we know.
The fact of weight makes it impossible
For everything to happen through collisions
(Or external force). But what prevents
The mind from moving by necessity

[290] And grinding through its own unchanging script,
Or moving automatically along,
Is just a hairline swerve among the atoms,
Unpredictable in time and place.

Book II.991–1104

Lucretius elaborates on the theory of multiple worlds, making explicit that it is intended to demonstrate how the universe (or multiverse) can operate without divine oversight.

We all spring forth from one celestial seed.
One father sheds his drops of liquid life
Onto the Earth, our mother, who receives them,
Gestates, and gives birth to luscious fruits,
Exultant trees, and us: the human race.
[995] She generates the many forms of beasts
And issues forth the sustenance they graze on,
Nourishing their bodies for a life
Of ease and procreation. These sweet gifts
Have rightly earned the Earth the name of "mother."
All that comes from her returns again,
[1000] And everything the air breathes forth returns

59

To be absorbed again and find its place
Within the heavenly dominions. Death
Can never physically destroy a thing
So fully that its matter vanishes.
Instead it breaks apart what once was fused,
Which then goes on to bond with other things,
Creating something else, with the result
That all the parts acquire different shapes
[1005] And change their colors, taking on new forms,
Acquiring consciousness and sentience
Then giving both up easily. This shows
The role of combination and position,
Which, when subtly altered, can transform
A limited array of elements
Into a varied range of different things.
[1010] Never imagine that the qualities
Which ripple on the outer surfaces
Of solid bodies could be permanent.
We watch them flicker into life and die.
See: even in these lines of poetry,
It matters what goes where, and next to what.
The same few letters can be used to mean
[1015] The sea, the air, the rivers, and the sun;
One set of characters can signify
The forests and the fields and all their fruits,
The birds and beasts. And though not every word
Contains the same amount or kind of letters,
Most of them will always be the same:
It's their arrangement that distinguishes
What thing each word denotes. And things themselves

Are similarly made from smaller parts.
When these material components change
[1020] Their relative positions, motions, bonds,
Configurations or trajectories,
The order or arrangement of their shapes,
The objects they compose must change as well.

Now stretch your mind; consider something new:
An unfamiliar truth is straining now
[1025] To gain a hearing and reveal its face.
But nothing is so simple to explain
That we can hear it once and instantly
Believe. But neither, on the other hand,
Is anything so strange and marvelous
That we don't grow accustomed over time.
Little by little everyone can learn
To take the most astounding facts in stride.
Consider first of all the clarity,
[1030] The pure and limpid color of the sky
And all that rests within it: roving stars
That wander through its vast expanse, the moon,
And, blazing with its searing light, the sun.
If mortal men had never seen all this
And found themselves confronted with it all
At once, and for the first time, what on earth
[1035] Could possibly be more astonishing?
What wouldn't they more readily believe?
Nothing, I think. That is how marvelous
The sight would be which now, from pure fatigue
Of daily viewing, never fazes us.

We hardly even think it's worth our time
To glance up at the heavenly domain.
[1040] In consequence, from now on, never let
The novelty of any strange idea
Suffice to spook you into shunning it.
Instead, double your efforts and attention;
Exercise your judgment to discern
Its merits. And if it seems true to you,
Lay down your weapons. Whereas if it's false,
Gear up to fight. My mind is on the hunt
For explanations of the farthest things
In regions of untraveled space, beyond
[1045] The walls that bound the world, where human
    thought
Bursts infinitely free, and flies at will
To seek and see whatever it can find.
First of all, everywhere, on every side
Of our position, to the left or right,
Or up or down, or any way at all,
[1050] There is no limit, as I have explained—
And as the facts themselves can plainly show,
For nature's yawning depths are evident.
Now then, since the infinite abyss
Expands in all directions endlessly,
And endlessly throughout this void there fly
Innumerable elements of things,
Perpetually moving, in no way
[1055] Should it be thought of as remotely true
That only this one orb of earth and air
Was ever made, and all those other atoms

Just do nothing in the void beyond—
Especially since this world came to be
By chance, a product of the laws of nature:
[1060] Raw matter was colliding pointlessly
And moving automatically, until
At last those atoms came together which,
Whenever they make contact, mix to form
The prime components of enormous things,
Setting in motion land and sea and sky,
And all the families of living things.
It follows and must also be confessed
[1065] That elsewhere other such material
Has mixed and mingled to create new worlds
Like this one here, which our Earth's atmosphere
Encircles and embraces jealously.
Moreover, where there is sufficient space
And matter in abundance, if no block
Or obstacle prevents it, things are bound
To happen: no surprises if they do.
[1070] And if the store of raw material
Is too enormous to be counted up
In all the lifetimes that were ever lived,
And those same laws of nature still endure
Which drive the raw materials to move
And which can still propel them to combine
In much the same ways as they have done here,
[1075] We must conclude that there are spheres
In other places, other lands and peoples,
Families and species, other beasts.
To these considerations we may add

The fact that in the whole extent of space
There's nothing that's unique or grows alone.
No creature is a species to itself:
Nature makes everything in generations,
[1080] Grouping them all together by their types.
So you will find the mountain-roving beasts
Are grouped this way, and so is humankind
(Dimorphic as it is), and so are fish,
Which swim in scaly schools, and flying birds.
We must conclude that this same principle
Holds also for the sky, the land and sun,
[1085] The moon and sea, the Earth, and all the rest.
These too are not unique, but numerous,
Innumerable, formed, like other things,
By fundamental laws of nature, which
Mark off the boundary stones of what can be.
If you can bear these things secure in mind,
Then nature will reveal herself to you
[1090] Exactly as she is: unfettered. Free.
She has no overbearing lords: alone,
Spontaneous, she does the things she does.
She knows no gods. For—by the gods themselves,
Who live eternal lives of peaceful bliss
With quiet hearts of pure serenity—
[1095] What god could rule the vastness of all things?
Whose hand is firm enough to hold the reins
And keep them steady, tame the endless deep?
Who could compass all the sky at once
And roll its spheres, while also stoking flames
From purest air to scour the whole earth?

Who can be everywhere at every time,
[1100] Shading the sky with clouds and shattering
Its silences with thunder, sending bolts
Of lightning down upon his own stone shrines,
Or else retreating to the desert wastes
For savage target practice, managing
To miss the mark and strike the innocent?

Book V.1028–90

Lucretius elaborates on the Epicurean theory of how language was formed—not through imposed convention by an original "namegiver," as for example in Plato's Cratylus, *but naturally and automatically, as a consequence of what we might call biological necessity and evolutionary development.*

Nature drove mankind to utter forth
The sounds of speech, and then convenience
Distinguished all the many names of things.
[1030] The situation wasn't so unlike
When children, immature in speech, are forced
To gesture mutely with their hands and point
At what they mean. For every living thing
Can sense the powers that it has to use.
A calf, before its horns have even sprouted,
Sticks its forehead out and thrusts at things

[1035] That make it angry. Little panther cubs
And lion whelps will snap and swipe and fight
With teeth and claws that aren't even grown.
Among the birds, all species, as we see,
Will test their wobbling wings and feeble feathers
[1040] Trusting in them for support. And so,
The mere idea that once upon a time
Some teacher handed out the names of things
And then instructed men in how to say them—
It's absurd. What gives us the idea
That this one man had all the sounds and words
[1045] To give at once to everything that is
When no one else could do so? Furthermore,
If others hadn't yet been using words
Among themselves, then how could he have known
The usefulness of speech, or gained the knack
For forming an idea to be expressed?
One man could never wrangle all the rest
[1050] Or force them to consent and settle down
Until they learned to use the names he chose.
Besides, he never could have taught the deaf,
By any easy means, the thing to do.
They never would have sat there and endured
[1055] To have their ears assaulted pointlessly
By useless sounds of words as yet unheard.
Besides, why *should* it be a mystery
If human beings, having tongues and voices,
Use their powers to convey in sound
The many things their senses can perceive,
Since even speechless wild animals

And even the domesticated beasts
[1060] Emit a varied range of different sounds
When fear or pain or joy suffuses them?
This can be demonstrated readily:
The minute mastiff hounds are spurred to rage,
They stretch their floppy lips into a snarl,
And bear their fearsome teeth, and make a noise
[1065] Quite different from the one they use to bark
And fill the neighborhood. And then again,
When licking at their pups, or cuffing them,
Or nipping playfully with teeth held back,
Pretending to devour them, their voice
[1070] Is whimpering and tender, quite distinct
From when they howl in the house alone
Or when they're beaten and they meekly whine.
Isn't it obvious with stallions
As well? They neigh and snort among the mares
[1075] When in their prime: Desire spurs them on,
Their nostrils flaring for the clash to come.
They sound quite different when some terror looms
And makes them quake and whinny. Finally,
The many types and kinds of winged birds—
The vultures and the hawks and ocean gulls
[1080] That hunt their prey amid the salty waves—
Make very different sounds at different times,
When fighting for their food or chasing it.
And some of them will sing a different song
Depending on the weather: ancient crows
[1085] And parliaments of rooks will call for rain
Or ask for wind and breezes with their cries.

So, if the animals, which cannot speak,
Still find themselves compelled to give forth voice
By various emotions and perceptions,
Early man must far more certainly
[1090] Have been equipped to utter many sounds.

PART III

The Age of Epicurus

Isaac Newton, *Opticks: Or, A Treatise of the Reflexions, Refractions, Inflexions and Colors of Light* (1704), from Question 31

In a feat of geometric reasoning and experimental observation, Newton demonstrated that the various colors of light exhibit different patterns of linear motion, most famously by passing white light through a prism to produce a rainbow. Here, he speculates that matter is not infinitely divisible but composed of atomic particles— interestingly, given what Einstein and the forefathers of quantum physics would later discover, Newton thought even light was made of "corpuscles" or indivisible particles.

All Bodies seem to be composed of hard Particles: For otherwise Fluids would not congeal; as Water, Oils, Vinegar, and Spirit or Oil of Vitriol do by freezing; Mercury by Fumes of Lead; Spirit of Nitre and Mercury, by dissolving the Mercury and evaporating the Flegm; Spirit of Wine and Spirit of Urine, by deflegming and

mixing them; and Spirit of Urine and Spirit of Salt, by subliming
them together to make Sal-armoniac. Even the Rays of Light seem
to be hard Bodies; for otherwise they would not retain different
Properties in their different Sides. And therefore Hardness may
be reckon'd the Property of all uncompounded Matter. At least,
this seems to be as evident as the universal Impenetrability of
Matter. For all Bodies, so far as Experience reaches, are either
hard, or may be harden'd; and we have no other Evidence of
universal Impenetrability, besides a large Experience without an
experimental Exception. Now if compound Bodies are so very
hard as we find some of them to be, and yet are very porous, and
consist of Parts which are only laid together; the simple Particles
which are void of Pores, and were never yet divided, must be
much harder. For such hard Particles being heaped up together,
can scarce touch one another in more than a few Points, and
therefore must be separable by much less Force than is requisite
to break a solid Particle, whose Parts touch in all the Space
between them, without any Pores or Interstices to weaken their
Cohesion. And how such very hard Particles which are only laid
together and touch only in a few Points, can stick together, and
that so firmly as they do, without the assistance of something
which causes them to be attracted or press'd towards one another,
is very difficult to conceive.

David Hume, *An Enquiry Concerning Human Understanding* (1748), Section XI: Of a Particular Providence and of a Future State

Hume makes Epicurus defend his belief that the orderly construction of nature offers no warrant for believing in an omnipotent or benevolent creator. He raises and disputes many of the typical objections to Epicureanism, including that it generates moral laxity. He also coyly suggests that his own argument might lead not simply to denying God's benevolence and omnipotence, but to denying his existence outright.

102. I was lately engaged in conversation with a friend who loves sceptical paradoxes; where, though he advanced many principles, of which I can by no means approve, yet as they seem to be curious, and to bear some relation to the chain of reasoning carried on throughout this enquiry, I shall here copy them from my

memory as accurately as I can, in order to submit them to the judgement of the reader.

Our conversation began with my admiring the singular good fortune of philosophy, which, as it requires entire liberty above all other privileges, and chiefly flourishes from the free opposition of sentiments and argumentation, received its first birth in an age and country of freedom and toleration, and was never cramped, even in its most extravagant principles, by any creeds, concessions, or penal statutes. For, except the banishment of Protagoras, and the death of Socrates, which last event proceeded partly from other motives, there are scarcely any instances to be met with, in ancient history, of this bigotted jealousy, with which the present age is so much infested. Epicurus lived at Athens to an advanced age, in peace and tranquillity: Epicureans were even admitted to receive the sacerdotal character, and to officiate at the altar, in the most sacred rites of the established religion: And the public encouragement of pensions and salaries was afforded equally, by the wisest of all the Roman emperors, to the professors of every sect of philosophy. How requisite such kind of treatment was to philosophy, in her early youth, will easily be conceived, if we reflect, that, even at present, when she may be supposed more hardy and robust, she bears with much difficulty the inclemency of the seasons, and those harsh winds of calumny and persecution, which blow upon her.

You admire, says my friend, as the singular good fortune of philosophy, what seems to result from the natural course of things, and to be unavoidable in every age and nation. This pertinacious bigotry, of which you complain, as so fatal to philosophy, is really her offspring, who, after allying with superstition, separates himself entirely from the interest of his parent, and becomes her most inveterate enemy and persecutor. Speculative dogmas of religion, the present occasions of such furious dispute, could not possibly be conceived or admitted in the early ages of the world; when mankind, being wholly illiterate, formed an idea of religion more suitable to their weak apprehension, and composed their sacred tenets of such tales chiefly as were the objects of traditional belief, more than of argument or disputation. After the first alarm, therefore, was over, which arose from the new paradoxes and principles of the philosophers; these teachers seem ever after, during the ages of antiquity, to have lived in great harmony with the established superstition, and to have made a fair partition of mankind between them; the former claiming all the learned and wise, the latter possessing all the vulgar and illiterate.

103. It seems then, say I, that you leave politics entirely out of the question, and never suppose, that a wise magistrate can justly be jealous of certain tenets of philosophy, such as those of Epicurus, which, denying a divine existence, and consequently a providence and a future state, seem to loosen, in a great measure, the ties of morality, and may be supposed, for that reason, pernicious to the peace of civil society.

I know, replied he, that in fact these persecutions never, in any age, proceeded from calm reason, or from experience of the pernicious consequences of philosophy; but arose entirely from passion and prejudice. But what if I should advance farther, and assert, that if Epicurus had been accused before the people, by any of the *sycophants* or informers of those days, he could easily have defended his cause, and proved his principles of philosophy to be as salutary as those of his adversaries, who endeavoured, with such zeal, to expose him to the public hatred and jealousy?

I wish, said I, you would try your eloquence upon so extraordinary a topic, and make a speech for Epicurus, which might satisfy, not the mob of Athens, if you will allow that ancient and polite city to have contained any mob, but the more philosophical part of his audience, such as might be supposed capable of comprehending his arguments.

The matter would not be difficult, upon such conditions, replied he: And if you please, I shall suppose myself Epicurus for a moment, and make you stand for the Athenian people, and shall deliver you such an harangue as will fill all the urn with white beans, and leave not a black one to gratify the malice of my adversaries.[1]

Very well: Pray proceed upon these suppositions.

104. I come hither, O ye Athenians, to justify in your assembly what I maintained in my school, and I find myself impeached by furious antagonists, instead of reasoning with calm and dispassionate enquirers. Your deliberations, which of right should be directed to questions of public good, and the interest of the commonwealth, are diverted to the disquisitions of speculative philosophy; and these magnificent, but perhaps fruitless enquiries, take place of your more familiar but more useful occupations. But so far as in me lies, I will prevent this abuse. We shall not here dispute concerning the origin and government of worlds. We shall only enquire how far such questions concern the public interest. And if I can persuade you, that they are entirely indifferent to the peace of society and security of government, I hope that you will presently send us back to our schools, there to

---

1   This refers to the ancient Greek practice of voting in political deliberations and court cases with white and black beans or pebbles.

examine, at leisure, the question the most sublime, but at the same time, the most speculative of all philosophy.

The religious philosophers, not satisfied with the tradition of your forefathers, and doctrine of your priests (in which I willingly acquiesce), indulge a rash curiosity, in trying how far they can establish religion upon the principles of reason; and they thereby excite, instead of satisfying, the doubts, which naturally arise from a diligent and scrutinous enquiry. They paint, in the most magnificent colours, the order, beauty, and wise arrangement of the universe; and then ask, if such a glorious display of intelligence could proceed from the fortuitous concourse of atoms, or if chance could produce what the greatest genius can never sufficiently admire. I shall not examine the justness of this argument. I shall allow it to be as solid as my antagonists and accusers can desire. It is sufficient, if I can prove, from this very reasoning, that the question is entirely speculative, and that, when, in my philosophical disquisitions, I deny a providence and a future state, I undermine not the foundations of society, but advance principles, which they themselves, upon their own topics, if they argue consistently, must allow to be solid and satisfactory.

105. You then, who are my accusers, have acknowledged, that the chief or sole argument for a divine existence (which I never questioned) is derived from the order of nature; where there appear such marks of intelligence and design, that you think it extravagant to assign for its cause, either chance, or the blind and unguided force of matter. You allow, that this is an argument drawn from effects to causes. From the order of the work, you infer, that there must have been project and forethought in the workman. If you cannot make out this point, you allow, that

your conclusion fails; and you pretend not to establish the conclusion in a greater latitude than the phenomena of nature will
justify. These are your concessions. I desire you to mark the
consequences.

When we infer any particular cause from an effect, we must
proportion the one to the other, and can never be allowed to
ascribe to the cause any qualities, but what are exactly sufficient
to produce the effect. A body of ten ounces raised in any scale
may serve as a proof, that the counterbalancing weight exceeds
ten ounces; but can never afford a reason that it exceeds a hundred. If the cause, assigned for any effect, be not sufficient to
produce it, we must either reject that cause, or add to it such
qualities as will give it a just proportion to the effect. But if we
ascribe to it farther qualities, or affirm it capable of producing
other effects, we can only indulge the licence of conjecture, and
arbitrarily suppose the existence of qualities and energies, without
reason or authority.

The same rule holds, whether the cause assigned be brute
unconscious matter, or a rational intelligent being. If the cause
be known only by the effect, we never ought to ascribe to it any
qualities, beyond what are precisely requisite to produce the
effect: Nor can we, by any rules of just reasoning, return back
from the cause, and infer other effects from it, beyond those by
which alone it is known to us. No one, merely from the sight of
one of Zeuxis's pictures, could know, that he was also a statuary
or architect, and was an artist no less skilful in stone and marble
than in colours. The talents and taste, displayed in the particular
work before us; these we may safely conclude the workman to be
possessed of. The cause must be proportioned to the effect; and
if we exactly and precisely proportion it, we shall never find in it

any qualities, that point farther, or afford an inference concerning any other design or performance. Such qualities must be somewhat beyond what is merely requisite for producing the effect, which we examine.

106. Allowing, therefore, the gods to be the authors of the existence or order of the universe; it follows, that they possess that precise degree of power, intelligence, and benevolence, which appears in their workmanship; but nothing farther can ever be proved, except we call in the assistance of exaggeration and flattery to supply the defects of argument and reasoning. So far as the traces of any attributes, at present, appear, so far may we conclude these attributes to exist. The supposition of farther attributes is mere hypothesis; much more the supposition, that, in distant regions of space or periods of time, there has been, or will be, a more magnificent display of these attributes, and a scheme of administration more suitable to such imaginary virtues. We can never be allowed to mount up from the universe, the effect, to Jupiter, the cause; and then descend downwards, to infer any new effect from that cause; as if the present effects alone were not entirely worthy of the glorious attributes, which we ascribe to that deity. The knowledge of the cause being derived solely from the effect, they must be exactly adjusted to each other; and the one can never refer to anything farther, or be the foundation of any new inference and conclusion.

You find certain phenomena in nature. You seek a cause or author. You imagine that you have found him. You afterwards become so enamoured of this offspring of your brain, that you imagine it impossible, but he must produce something greater and more perfect than the present scene of things, which is so full of ill and disorder. You forget, that this superlative intelligence and benevolence are entirely imaginary, or, at least, without any foundation in reason; and that you have no ground to ascribe to him any qualities, but what you see he has actually exerted and displayed in his productions. Let your gods, therefore, O philosophers, be suited to the present appearances of nature: and presume not to alter these appearances by arbitrary suppositions, in order to suit them to the attributes, which you so fondly ascribe to your deities.

107. When priests and poets, supported by your authority, O Athenians, talk of a golden or silver age, which preceded the present state of vice and misery, I hear them with attention and with reverence. But when philosophers, who pretend to neglect authority, and to cultivate reason, hold the same discourse, I pay them not, I own, the same obsequious submission and pious deference. I ask; who carried them into the celestial regions, who admitted them into the councils of the gods, who opened to them the book of fate, that they thus rashly affirm, that their deities have executed, or will execute, any purpose beyond what has actually appeared? If they tell me, that they have mounted on the steps or by the gradual ascent of reason, and by drawing inferences from effects to causes, I still insist, that they have aided the ascent of reason by the wings of imagination; otherwise they could not thus change their manner of inference, and argue from causes to effects; presuming, that a more perfect production than the present world would be more suitable to such perfect beings as the gods, and forgetting that they have no reason to ascribe to these celestial beings any perfection or any attribute, but what can be found in the present world.

Hence all the fruitless industry to account for the ill appearances of nature, and save the honour of the gods; while we must acknowledge the reality of that evil and disorder, with which the world so much abounds. The obstinate and intractable qualities of matter, we are told, or the observance of general laws, or some such reason, is the sole cause, which controlled the power and benevolence of Jupiter, and obliged him to create mankind and every sensible creature so imperfect and so unhappy. These attributes then, are, it seems, beforehand, taken for granted, in their greatest latitude. And upon that supposition, I own that such conjectures may, perhaps, be admitted as plausible solutions of the ill phenomena. But still I ask; Why take these attributes for granted, or why ascribe to the cause any qualities but what actually appear in the effect? Why torture your brain to justify the course of nature upon suppositions, which, for aught you know, may be entirely imaginary, and of which there are to be found no traces in the course of nature?

The religious hypothesis, therefore, must be considered only as a particular method of accounting for the visible phenomena of the universe: but no just reasoner will ever presume to infer from it any single fact, and alter or add to the phenomena, in any single particular. If you think, that the appearances of things prove such causes, it is allowable for you to draw an inference concerning the existence of these causes. In such complicated and sublime subjects, every one should be indulged in the liberty of conjecture and argument. But here you ought to rest. If you come backward, and arguing from your inferred causes, conclude, that any other fact has existed, or will exist, in the course of nature, which may serve as a fuller display of particular attributes; I must admonish you, that you have departed from the method of reasoning, attached to the present subject, and have certainly added something to the attributes of the cause, beyond what appears in the effect; otherwise you could never, with tolerable sense or

propriety, add anything to the effect, in order to render it more
worthy of the cause.

108. Where, then, is the odiousness of that doctrine, which
I teach in my school, or rather, which I examine in my gardens?
Or what do you find in this whole question, wherein the security
of good morals, or the peace and order of society, is in the least
concerned?

I deny a providence, you say, and supreme governor of the
world, who guides the course of events, and punishes the vicious
with infamy and disappointment, and rewards the virtuous with
honour and success, in all their undertakings. But surely, I deny
not the course itself of events, which lies open to every one's
inquiry and examination. I acknowledge, that, in the present order
of things, virtue is attended with more peace of mind than vice,
and meets with a more favourable reception from the world. I am
sensible, that, according to the past experience of mankind, friendship is the chief joy of human life, and moderation the only source
of tranquillity and happiness. I never balance between the virtuous
and the vicious course of life; but am sensible, that, to a
well-disposed mind, every advantage is on the side of the former.
And what can you say more, allowing all your suppositions and
reasonings? You tell me, indeed, that this disposition of things
proceeds from intelligence and design. But whatever it proceeds
from, the disposition itself, on which depends our happiness or
misery, and consequently our conduct and deportment in life is
still the same. It is still open for me, as well as you, to regulate my
behaviour, by my experience of past events. And if you affirm,
that, while a divine providence is allowed, and a supreme distributive justice in the universe, I ought to expect some more particular
reward of the good, and punishment of the bad, beyond the

ordinary course of events; I here find the same fallacy, which I have before endeavoured to detect. You persist in imagining, that, if we grant that divine existence, for which you so earnestly contend, you may safely infer consequences from it, and add something to the experienced order of nature, by arguing from the attributes which you ascribe to your gods. You seem not to remember, that all your reasonings on this subject can only be drawn from effects to causes; and that every argument, deducted from causes to effects, must of necessity be a gross sophism; since it is impossible for you to know anything of the cause, but what you have antecedently, not inferred, but discovered to the full, in the effect.

109. But what must a philosopher think of those vain reasoners, who, instead of regarding the present scene of things as the sole object of their contemplation, so far reverse the whole course of nature, as to render this life merely a passage to something farther; a porch, which leads to a greater, and vastly different building; a prologue, which serves only to introduce the piece, and give it more grace and propriety? Whence, do you think, can such philosophers derive their idea of the gods? From their own conceit and imagination surely. For if they derived it from the present phenomena, it would never point to anything farther, but must be exactly adjusted to them. That the divinity may *possibly* be endowed with attributes, which we have never seen exerted; may be governed by principles of action, which we cannot discover to be satisfied: all this will freely be allowed. But still this is mere *possibility* and hypothesis. We never can have reason to *infer* any attributes, or any principles of action in him, but so far as we know them to have been exerted and satisfied.

Are there any marks of a distributive justice in the world? If you answer in the affirmative, I conclude, that, since justice here exerts itself, it is satisfied. If you reply in the negative, I conclude, that you have then no reason to ascribe justice, in our sense of it, to the gods. If you hold a medium between affirmation and negation, by saying, that the justice of the gods, at present, exerts itself in part, but not in its full extent; I answer, that you have no reason to give it any particular extent, but only so far as you see it, *at present*, exert itself.

110. Thus I bring the dispute, O Athenians, to a short issue with my antagonists. The course of nature lies open to my contemplation as well as to theirs. The experienced train of events is the great standard, by which we all regulate our conduct. Nothing else can be appealed to in the field, or in the senate. Nothing else ought ever to be heard of in the school, or in the closet. In vain would our limited understanding break through those boundaries, which are too narrow for our fond imagination. While we argue from the course of nature, and infer a particular intelligent cause, which first bestowed, and still preserves order in the universe, we embrace a principle, which is both uncertain and useless. It is uncertain; because the subject lies entirely beyond the reach of human experience. It is useless; because our knowledge of this cause being derived entirely from the course of nature, we can never, according to the rules of just reasoning, return back from the cause with any new inference, or making additions to the common and experienced course of nature, establish any new principles of conduct and behaviour.

111. I observe (said I, finding he had finished his harangue) that you neglect not the artifice of the demagogues of old; and as you were pleased to make me stand for the people, you insinuate yourself into my favour by embracing those principles, to which, you know, I have always expressed a particular attachment. But allowing you to make experience (as indeed I think you ought) the only standard of our judgement concerning this, and all other questions of fact; I doubt not but, from the very same experience, to which you appeal, it may be possible to refute this reasoning, which you have put into the mouth of Epicurus. If you saw, for instance, a half-finished building, surrounded with heaps of brick and stone and mortar, and all the instruments of masonry; could you not *infer* from the effect, that it was a work of design and contrivance? And could you not return again, from this inferred cause, to infer new additions to the effect, and conclude, that the building would soon be finished, and receive all the further improvements, which art could bestow upon it? If you saw upon the sea-shore the print of one human foot, you would conclude, that a man had passed that way, and that he had also left the traces of the other foot, though effaced by the rolling of the sands or inundation of the waters. Why then do you refuse to admit the same method of reasoning with regard to the order of nature? Consider the world and the present life only as an imperfect building, from which you can infer a superior intelligence; and arguing from that superior intelligence, which can leave nothing imperfect; why may you not infer a more finished scheme or plan, which will receive its completion in some distant point of space or time? Are not these methods of reasoning exactly similar? And under what pretence can you embrace the one, while you reject the other?

112. The infinite difference of the subjects, replied he, is a sufficient foundation for this difference in my conclusions. In works of *human* art and contrivance, it is allowable to advance from the effect to the cause, and returning back from the cause, to form new inferences concerning the effect, and examine the alterations,

which it has probably undergone, or may still undergo. But what is the foundation of this method of reasoning? Plainly this; that man is a being, whom we know by experience, whose motives and designs we are acquainted with, and whose projects and inclinations have a certain connexion and coherence, according to the laws which nature has established for the government of such a creature. When, therefore, we find, that any work has proceeded from the skill and industry of man; as we are otherwise acquainted with the nature of the animal, we can draw a hundred inferences concerning what may be expected from him; and these inferences will all be founded in experience and observation. But did we know man only from the single work or production which we examine, it were impossible for us to argue in this manner; because our knowledge of all the qualities, which we ascribe to him, being in that case derived from the production, it is impossible they could point to anything farther, or be the foundation of any new inference. The print of a foot in the sand can only prove, when considered alone, that there was some figure adapted to it, by which it was produced: but the print of a human foot proves likewise, from our other experience, that there was probably another foot, which also left its impression, though effaced by time or other accidents. Here we mount from the effect to the cause; and descending again from the cause, infer alterations in the effect; but this is not a continuation of the same simple chain of reasoning. We comprehend in this case a hundred other experiences and observations, concerning the *usual* figure and members of that species of animal, without which this method of argument must be considered as fallacious and sophistical.

113. The case is not the same with our reasonings from the works of nature. The Deity is known to us only by his

productions, and is a single being in the universe, not comprehended under any species or genus, from whose experienced attributes or qualities, we can, by analogy, infer any attribute or quality in him. As the universe shews wisdom and goodness, we infer
wisdom and goodness. As it shews a particular degree of these
perfections, we infer a particular degree of them, precisely adapted
to the effect which we examine. But farther attributes or farther
degrees of the same attributes, we can never be authorised to infer
or suppose, by any rules of just reasoning. Now, without some
such licence of supposition, it is impossible for us to argue from
the cause, or infer any alteration in the effect, beyond what has
immediately fallen under our observation. Greater good produced
by this Being must still prove a greater degree of goodness: a more
impartial distribution of rewards and punishments must proceed
from a greater regard to justice and equity. Every supposed addition to the works of nature makes an addition to the attributes
of the Author of nature; and consequently, being entirely unsup-
ported by any reason or argument, can never be admitted but as
mere conjecture and hypothesis.

The great source of our mistake in this subject, and of the
unbounded licence of conjecture, which we indulge, is, that we
tacitly consider ourselves, as in the place of the Supreme Being,
and conclude, that he will, on every occasion, observe the same
conduct, which we ourselves, in his situation, would have
embraced as reasonable and eligible. But, besides that the ordinary course of nature may convince us, that almost everything is
regulated by principles and maxims very different from ours;
besides this, I say, it must evidently appear contrary to all rules
of analogy to reason, from the intentions and projects of men, to
those of a Being so different, and so much superior. In human

nature, there is a certain experienced coherence of designs and inclinations; so that when, from any fact, we have discovered one intention of any man, it may often be reasonable, from experience, to infer another, and draw a long chain of conclusions concerning his past or future conduct. But this method of reasoning can never have place with regard to a Being, so remote and incomprehensible, who bears much less analogy to any other being in the universe than the sun to a waxen taper, and who discovers himself only by some faint traces or outlines, beyond which we have no authority to ascribe to him any attribute or perfection. What we imagine to be a superior perfection, may really be a defect. Or were it ever so much a perfection, the ascribing of it to the Supreme Being, where it appears not to have been really exerted, to the full, in his works, savours more of flattery and panegyric, than of just reasoning and sound philosophy. All the philosophy, therefore, in the world, and all the religion, which is nothing but a species of philosophy, will never be able to carry us beyond the usual course of experience, or give us measures of conduct and behaviour different from those which are furnished by reflections on common life. No new fact can ever be inferred from the religious hypothesis; no event foreseen or foretold; no reward or punishment expected or dreaded, beyond what is already known by practice and observation. So that my apology for Epicurus will still appear solid and satisfactory; nor have the political interests of society any connexion with the philosophical disputes concerning metaphysics and religion.

114. There is still one circumstance, replied I, which you seem to have overlooked. Though I should allow your premises, I must deny your conclusion. You conclude, that religious doctrines and reasonings *can* have no influence on life, because they *ought* to

have no influence; never considering, that men reason not in the same manner you do, but draw many consequences from the belief of a divine Existence, and suppose that the Deity will inflict punishments on vice, and bestow rewards on virtue, beyond what appear in the ordinary course of nature. Whether this reasoning of theirs be just or not, is no matter. Its influence on their life and conduct must still be the same. And, those, who attempt to disabuse them of such prejudices, may, for aught I know, be good reasoners, but I cannot allow them to be good citizens and politicians; since they free men from one restraint upon their passions, and make the infringement of the laws of society, in one respect, more easy and secure.

After all, I may, perhaps, agree to your general conclusion in favour of liberty, though upon different premises from those, on which you endeavour to found it. I think, that the state ought to tolerate every principle of philosophy; nor is there an instance, that any government has suffered in its political interests by such indulgence. There is no enthusiasm among philosophers; their doctrines are not very alluring to the people; and no restraint can be put upon their reasonings, but what must be of dangerous consequence to the sciences, and even to the state, by paving the way for persecution and oppression in points, where the generality of mankind are more deeply interested and concerned.

115. But there occurs to me (continued I) with regard to your main topic, a difficulty, which I shall just propose to you without insisting on it; lest it lead into reasonings of too nice and delicate a nature. In a word, I much doubt whether it be possible for a cause to be known only by its effect (as you have all along supposed) or to be of so singular and particular a nature as to have no parallel and no similarity with any other cause or object, that has ever fallen under our observation. It is only when two *species* of objects are found to be constantly conjoined, that we can infer the one from the other; and were an effect presented, which was entirely singular, and could not be comprehended under any known *species*, I do not see, that we could form any conjecture or inference at all concerning its cause. If experience and observation and analogy be, indeed, the only guides which we can reasonably follow in inferences of this nature; both the effect and cause must bear a similarity and resemblance to other effects and causes, which we know, and which we have found, in many instances, to be conjoined with each other. I leave it to your own reflection to pursue the consequences of this principle. I shall just observe, that, as the antagonists of Epicurus always suppose the universe, an effect quite singular and unparalleled, to be the proof of a Deity, a cause no less singular and unparalleled; your reasonings, upon that supposition, seem, at least, to merit our attention. There is, I own, some difficulty, how we can ever return from the cause to the effect, and, reasoning from our ideas of the former, infer any alteration on the latter, or any addition to it.

John Adams, *Letter to John Rogers, February 6, 1801*

The following two letters underscore how intensely America's founders discussed the philosophies of the Hellenistic schools, which they took to be serious contenders for the soul of their new nation. Adams sounds a lot like his role model, Cicero, in his contempt for all things Epicurean. By contrast, Jefferson's summary of his own beliefs neatly illustrates Adams's point that some variety of Epicureanism is recognizably the default position of many moderns.

Dear Sir,
I thank you for your kind letter of Jan 31st. If the judiciary bill should pass, as I hope it will, it will cost me much anxiety and dilligence, to select characters such as you describe to fill the offices & I am obliged to you & to all other friends of their Country, who favor me with their advice & assistance in discharging that important duty. I have a personal regard for Mr. Bayard & his father has been long my friend, but I can make no promise, nor give any

encouragement untill all the candidates are before me & I have taken time to weigh their qualifications & merits. I have no doubt he deserves the handsome character you give him. The character "of an ennemy to the fatal philosophy of the day" has great weight with me, although it appears to have none with our nation. But I shall not dilate on this head. It behoves all men to consider whether that intelligence & piety and virtue in the great body of the people, upon which we have all acknowledged our whole security to depend, has not failed our expectations & disappointed all our hopes. We in this age are more unfortunate in one respect than the ancient gentiles. Among them the philosophers were divided into numerous sects—the folowers of Socrates of Plato of Pythagoras & of Zeno as well as of Epicurus. All the former had a mixture of good morals, manly virtues & true opinions among their errors & all of them served to counterpoise & counteract the poisonous pestilential & most fatal doctrine of Epicurus. The portico for example produced men like the Catoes, Cicero, Seneca, Brutus, Epictetus and others who were saints in comparison of Caesar and Anthony. But our modern philosophers are all the low grovelling disciples of Epicurus: Not one Stoick no Platonician among them. Where then are we going! Are we all to become *Epicuri de grege porci*?[1]—There is one thing, My dear Doctor, which has given me much uneasiness. How can it have happened that such great numbers of our good friends the Presbyterians have become the advocates, disciples & voters, if not votaries of the great doctors of Epicurean phylosophy? But I have written a tedious letter when I intended only to have acknowledged your favor.

   With much esteem I am Sir your friend & humble ser[vant].

---

1   "Pigs from Epicurus's herd"

Thomas Jefferson, *Letter to William Short,*
October 31, 1819

Dear Sir,

Your favor of the 21st is received. my late illness, in which you are
so kind as to feel an interest was produced by a spasmodic stric-
ture of the ilium, which came upon me on the 7th inst. the crisis
was short, passed over favorably on the 4th day, and I should soon
have been well but that a dose of calomel & Jalap, in which were
only 8. or 9. grains of the former brought on a salivation. of this
however nothing now remains but a little soreness of the mouth.
I have been able to get on horseback for 3. or 4. days past.

As you say of yourself, I too am an Epicurean. I consider
the genuine (not the imputed) doctrines of Epicurus as containing every thing rational in moral philosophy which Greece &
Rome have left us. Epictetus indeed has given us what was good
of the Stoics; all beyond, of their dogmas, being hypocrisy and
grimace. their great crime was in their calumnies of Epicurus

and misrepresentations of his doctrines: in which we lament to
see the candid character of Cicero engaging as an accomplice.
the merit of his philosophy is in the beauties of his style. diffuse,
vapid, rhetorical, but enchanting. his prototype Plato, eloquent
as himself, dealing out mysticisms incomprehensible to the
human mind, has been deified by certain sects usurping the
name of Christians; because, in his foggy conceptions, they
found a basis of impenetrable darkness whereon to rear fabrications as delirious, of their own invention. these they fathered
blasphemously on him whom they claimed as their founder, but
who would disclaim them with the indignation which their
caricatures of his religion so justly excite. of Socrates we have
nothing genuine but in the Memorabilia of Xenophon. for Plato
makes him one of his Collocutors merely to cover his own
whimsies under the mantle of his name; a liberty of which we
are told Socrates himself complained. Seneca is indeed a fine
moralist, disfiguring his work at times with some Stoicisms, and
affecting too much of antithesis and point, yet giving us on the
whole a great deal of sound and practical morality. but the greatest of all the Reformers of the depraved religion of his own
country, was Jesus of Nazareth. abstracting what is really his
from the rubbish in which it is buried, easily distinguished by
its lustre from the dross of his biographers, and as separable
from that as the diamond from the dung hill, we have the outlines of a system of the most sublime morality which has ever
fallen from the lips of man: outlines which it is lamentable he
did not live to fill up. Epictetus & Epicurus give us laws for
governing ourselves, Jesus a supplement of the duties & charities
we owe to others. the establishment of the innocent and genuine
character of this benevolent Moralist, and the rescuing it from

the imputation of imposture, which has resulted from artificial systems, invented by Ultra-Christian sects, unauthorised by a single word ever uttered by him is a most desirable object, and one to which Priestly has succesfully devoted his labors and learning. it would in time, it is to be hoped, effect a quiet euthanasia of the heresies of bigotry and fanaticism which have so long triumphed over human reason, and so generally & deeply afflicted mankind. but this work is to be begun by winnowing the grain from the chaff of the historians of his life. I have sometimes thought of translating Epictetus (for he has never been tolerably translated into English) of adding the genuine doctrines of Epicurus from the Syntagma of Gassendi, and an Abstract from the Evangelists of whatever has the stamp of the eloquence and fine imagination of Jesus. the last I attempted too hastily some 12. or 15. years ago. it was the work of 2. or 3. nights only at Washington, after getting thro' the evening task of reading the letters and papers of the day.——but with one foot in the grave, these are now idle projects for me. my business is to beguile the wearisomness of declining life, as I endeavor to do, by the delights of classical reading and of Mathematical truths, and by the consolations of a sound philosophy, equally indifferent to hope & fear.

I take the liberty of observing that you are not a true disciple of our master Epicurus, in indulging the indolence to which you say you are yielding. one of his canons, you know, was that 'that indulgence which prevents a greater pleasure, or produces a greater pain, is to be avoided.' your love of repose will lead, in its progress, to a suspension of healthy exercise, a relaxation of mind, an indifference to every thing around you, and finally to a debility of body and hebetude of mind, the farthest of all things from the happiness which the well regulated indulgences of Epicurus ensure. fortitude, you know, is one of his four cardinal virtues. that teaches us to meet and surmount difficulties; not to fly from them, like cowards. and to fly too in vain, for they will meet and arrest us at every turn of our road. weigh this matter well; brace yourself up; take a seat with Correa, and come and see the finest portion of your country which, if you have not forgotten, you still do not know, because it is no longer the same as when you knew it. it will add much to the happiness of my recovery to be able to receive Correa and yourself, and to prove the estimation in which I hold you both. come too and see our incipient University, which has advanced with great activity this year. by the end of the next we shall have elegant accomodations for 7. professors, & the year following the professors themselves. no secondary character will be received among them. either the ablest which America or Europe can furnish, or none at all. they will give us the selected society of a great city separated from the dissipations and levities of its ephemeral insects.

I am glad the bust of Condorcet has been saved and so well placed. his genius should be before us; while the lamentable, but singular act of ingratitude, which tarnished his latter days, may be thrown behind us.

I will place under this a Syllabus of the doctrines of Epicurus, somewhat in the lapidary style, which I wrote some 20. years ago. a like one of the philosophy of Jesus, of nearly the same age, is too long to be copied.

Vale, et tibi persuade carissimum te esse mihi.[1]

---

1   "Farewell, and be assured that you are most dear to me."

Enclosure: A Syllabus of the doctrines of Epicurus.

Physical.

The Universe eternal.

its parts, great & small, interchangeable.

Matter and Void alone.

Motion inherent in matter, which is weighty & declining.

eternal circulation of the elements of bodies.

Gods, an order of beings next superior to man.

enjoying, in their sphere, their own felicities;

but not medling with the concerns of the scale of beings below them.

Moral.

Happiness the aim of life.

Virtue the foundation of happiness;

Utility the test of virtue.

Pleasure active and In-dolent.

In-dolence is the absence of pain, the true felicity.

Active, consists in agreeable motion

it is not happiness. but the means to produce it.

thus the absence of hunger is an article of felicity; eating the means to obtain it.

The Summum bonum is to be not pained in body, nor troubled in mind.

i.e. **In-dolence** of body, tranquility of mind.

to procure tranquility of mind we must avoid **desire** & **fear** the two principal diseases of the mind.

Man is a free agent.

Virtue consists in   1. Prudence 2. Temperance 3. Fortitude 4. Justice

to which are opposed 1. Folly   2. Desire   3. Fear   4. Deciept

James Clerk Maxwell, *selections from "Molecules,"* in Nature 8 (1873), 437–441

Originally delivered as a lecture to the British Association at Bradford, this essay proposes that atoms are the most enduring and stable components of a universe designed by God, intriguingly blending Epicurean physics with more traditional Christian theology. Between the two, it's the latter that has fared better as a way of understanding the world. The former collapsed shortly after this lecture was delivered—in part, ironically, on the basis of what Einstein learned from Maxwell's own discoveries.

... Take any portion of matter, say a drop of water, and observe its properties. Like every other portion of matter we have ever seen, it is divisible. Divide it in two, each portion appears to retain all the properties of the original drop, and among others that of being divisible. The parts are similar to the whole in every respect except in absolute size.

Now go on repeating the process of division till the separate portions of water are so small that we can no longer perceive or handle them. Still we have no doubt that the sub-division might be carried further, if our senses were more acute and our instruments more delicate. Thus far all are agreed, but now the question arises, Can this sub-division be repeated for ever?

According to Democritus and the atomic school, we must answer in the negative. After a certain number of sub-divisions, the drop would be divided into a number of parts each of which is incapable of further sub-division. We should thus, in imagination, arrive at the atom, which, as its name literally signifies, cannot be cut in two. This is the atomic doctrine of Democritus, Epicurus, and Lucretius, and, I may add, of your lecturer.

•   •   •

When Lucretius wishes us to form a mental representation of the motion of atoms, he tells us to look at a sunbeam shining through a darkened room (the same instrument of research by which Dr. Tyndall makes visible to us the dust we breathe) and to observe the motes which chase each other in all directions through it. This motion of the visible motes, he tells us, is but a result of the far more complicated motion of the invisible atoms which knock the motes about. In his dream of nature, as Tennyson tells us, he "saw the flaring atom-streams And torrents of her myriad universe, Ruining along the illimitable inane, Fly on to clash together again, and make Another and another frame of things For ever."

And it is no wonder that he should have attempted to burst the bonds of Fate by making his atoms deviate from their Courses at quite uncertain times and places, thus attributing to them a kind of irrational free will, which on his materialistic theory is the only explanation of that power of voluntary action of which we ourselves are conscious.

• • •

Each molecule, therefore, throughout the universe, bears impressed on it the stamp of a metric system as distinctly as does the metre of the Archives at Paris, or the double royal cubit of the Temple of Karnac.

No theory of evolution can be formed to account for the similarity of molecules, for evolution necessarily implies continuous change, and the molecule is incapable of growth or decay, of generation or destruction.

None of the processes of Nature, since the time when Nature began, have produced the slightest difference in the properties of any molecule. We are therefore unable to ascribe either the existence of the molecules or the identity of their properties to the operation of any of the causes which we call natural.

On the other hand, the exact equality of each molecule to all others of the same kind gives it, as Sir John Herschel has well said, the essential character of a manufactured article, and precludes the idea of its being eternal and self existent.

Thus we have been led, along a strictly scientific path, very near to the point at which Science must stop. Not that Science is debarred from studying the internal mechanism of a molecule which she cannot take to pieces, any more than from investigating an organism which she cannot put together. But in tracing back the history of matter Science is arrested when she assures herself, on the one hand, that the molecule has been made, and on the other that it has not been made by any of the processes we call natural.

Science is incompetent to reason upon the creation of matter itself out of nothing. We have reached the utmost limit of our thinking faculties when we have admitted that because matter cannot be eternal and self-existent it must have been created.

It is only when we contemplate, not matter in itself, but the form in which it actually exists, that our mind finds something on which it can lay hold.

That matter, as such, should have certain fundamental properties—that it should exist in space and be capable of motion, that its motion should be persistent, and so on, are truths which may, for anything we know, be of the kind which metaphysicians call necessary. We may use our knowledge of such truths for purposes of deduction but we have no data for speculating as to their origin.

But that there should be exactly so much matter and no more in every molecule of hydrogen is a fact of a very different order. We have here a particular distribution of matter—a *collocation*—to use the expression of Dr. Chalmers, of things which we have no difficulty in imagining to have been arranged otherwise.

The form and dimensions of the orbits of the planets, for instance, are not determined by any law of nature, but depend upon a particular collocation of matter. The same is the case with respect to the size of the earth, from which the standard of what is called the metrical system has been derived. But these astronomical and terrestrial magnitudes are far inferior in scientific importance to that most fundamental of all standards which forms the base of the molecular system. Natural causes, as we know, are at work, which tend to modify, if they do not at length destroy, all the arrangements and dimensions of the earth and the whole solar system. But though in the course of ages catastrophes have occurred and may yet occur in the heavens, though ancient systems may be dissolved and new systems evolved out of their ruins, the molecules out of which these systems are built—the foundation stones of the material universe—remain unbroken and unworn.

They continue this day as they were created, perfect in number and measure and weight, and from the ineffaceable characters impressed on them we may learn that those aspirations after accuracy in measurement, truth in statement, and justice in action, which we reckon among our noblest attributes as men, are ours because they are essential constituents of the image of Him Who in the beginning created, not only the heaven and the earth, but the materials of which heaven and earth consist.

INDEX

inference on the order of
nature, xx, 79–80, 81, 83,
85–86, 87, 88, 89, 90, 92
philosophical study
in ancient culture, 76
detractors and paradoxes
of, 76–77, 78, 86, 92
priests/poets vs, 82, 83
plausible solutions of ill
phenomena, 83
religious philosophers
afterlife, 85
doctrinal influence on
society, 90–91
"effect before cause"
reasoning flaws, 79–81,
82, 83–84, 85, 91–92
hypothetical nature of
gods, 81–83
superlative intelligence
(Deity)
existence as lack of proof
for, 92
as imaginary, 86
inferred superiority
impossible to know,
88–89
man imposing own
attributes on, 81–82,
89–90

visible phenomena, 83
works of human art cause/
effect, 87–88
animals, 18, 37, 64, 67–69
Aristotle, xiii–xiv
art, 87–88
ataraxia (as Epicurean goal).
see also Menoeceus, letter to
(Epicurus)
bliss, xvii, xxi, 19, 40
goal of blessed life, 42–43,
44–45
happiness, 37, 40, 84, 99
hedonism/indulgence vs, xv,
xvii, xxi–xxii, xxxi, 43–44
inner peace, xvii, 29
peace of mind, xvii, xxxi,
25, 84
pleasure, xvii, xxi–xxii, xxx,
xxxi, 42–44, 84
serenity, viii, xvii, xxi–xxii,
xxx, 2, 20–21, 42
simple pleasures vs excess,
97–98, 99
virtues, xxi–xxii, 39, 44, 84,
94, 99
atheism, xxvi
Athenian thought, xiii–xiv,
77–78
atomos, xi